Scriptures for the

$\mathcal{L}$ent *2006*
Watch and Pray

A Lenten Study Based on the Revised Common Lectionary

Lee Franklin

ABINGDON PRESS

Nashville

Scriptures for the Church Seasons

A Study Book

WATCH AND PRAY

by Lee Franklin

Copyright © 2006 by Abingdon Press

Scripture quotations in this publication, unless otherwise indicated, are from the New Revised Standard Version of the Bible, copyright © 1989 by the Division of Christian Education of the National Council of the Churches of Christ in the United States of America, and are used by permission. All rights reserved.

All readings taken from the Revised Common Lectionary © 1992 Consultation on Common Texts are used by permission.

ISBN 0-687-35884-1

Manufactured in the United States of America

06   07   08   09   10   11   12   13   14   15—10   9   8   7   6   5   4   3   2   1

Contents

Introduction

The theme of this book is *Watch and Pray*—imperatives that seem simple and straightforward; but are they? What does it mean to watch and pray?

Our society emphasizes different kinds of watchfulness: watching out for one's own interests, watching TV to be distracted or entertained, watching Madison Avenue to see what is a "necessity," watching what others are buying or doing. For Christians, though, *to watch* takes on a different meaning.

Our society emphasizes a prayer of sorts. We are encouraged to ask for or demand what we want. We live in an age of instant gratification. It would be easy to think of prayer as asking the holder of the great charge card in the sky for what we want. Grace would be never receiving a bill. For Christians, though, *to pray* takes on a different meaning.

In the biblical tradition, watching and praying are associated with encountering God's loving, liberating, life-giving nature and purposes. We study Scripture so we can learn to recognize God's nature and purposes. We pray so that we may continually be shaped into the kind of people who participate in what God is doing in our lives, our churches, and our world.

The lectionary texts in the following chapters help to reveal God's nature and purposes. We will learn about God's covenantal promises for the good of creation. We will see the radical response God's promises inspire. We will study the Flood, seeing the difference perspective can make. We will examine the Exodus and find ways that God delivers us from oppressive powers. We will study the Exile and see what we can learn from this time of judgment and salvation. We will visit the spiritual disciplines, finding ways that we can place ourselves in a position to be blessed. We will discuss reasons to be faithful during difficult circumstances. We will examine the difficulties discipleship can present. Through it all, we will never lose sight of Jesus' resurrection and the promises of life, love, liberation, and salvation that it holds for all.

For Christians, Lent is a time to examine our hearts and our lives in order that we may be more fully shaped to participate in God's purposes. Let us watch and pray for a fruitful Lenten journey.

Seeing Things Differently

Scriptures for Lent:
The First Sunday
Genesis 9:8-17
1 Peter 3:18-22
Mark 1:9-15

Before getting out of bed, I looked out my window to see if the predicted snow had come. It had. A thick blanket of white covered the back yard. Wet flakes continued to fall from the ominous gray sky. I looked up to see the crystallized branches of huge oak trees arching achingly toward the ground. Their sparkle was lost on me.

Memories from the ice storm two years before were still sharp. Over the entire city, ice-heavy branches had come crashing down, damaging houses (ours among them), stripping power lines, and knocking out power for up to ten days. After surveying the present circumstances, I started gathering candles before even putting on my slippers.

When my sons awoke, they, too, looked out their windows. However, instead of seeing looming danger, they saw a good chance for a snow day, a day off from school. I was reminded that beauty (or looming tragedy) is in the eye of the beholder. What we see is often determined by our perspective.

Each of us knows what it means to face storms in life. The death of a loved one, illness, depression, relational discord, divorce, job struggles, and financial challenges are ones we may weather. War, poverty, hunger, war, terrorism, disease, and disaster ominously cloud the global horizon. The question: As we deal with what life sends our way, how do we view our surrounding circumstances? Through the lens of fear or through the lens of faith?

Our three texts this first week of Lent can inform and inspire a faithful perspective. Genesis 9:8-17 highlights God's covenant with creation, allowing us to see all of life, even times of chaos, in the light of God's promise. First Peter 3:18-22 offers perspective on suffering that a life of faith can entail. Mark 1:9-15 illuminates Jesus' identity and purposes as the Son of God commissioned to manifest the good news of God's kingdom.

These passages help us not only to *see* differently but also to *be* different. They help us to watch for what God is doing and to pray that we may more fully participate in God's life-giving purposes.

A MATTER OF PERSPECTIVE
Genesis 9:8-17

When I viewed the icy limbs out my window, I feared that all would soon come crashing down around me. It is natural to view a crisis, or perceived crisis, through the lens of fear; but our first text offers a different perspective.

The Flood story in Genesis 7–9 gives evidence of having been written during a time of profound crisis for the people of Judah. After Babylon conquered Jerusalem and destroyed the Temple in 587 B.C., circumstances seemed particularly bad for the people of Yahweh in exile (587-39 B.C.). They had lost their Temple—their primary place of encounter with God. They had lost the land God had given them. Worst of all, they thought they were in danger of losing their identity as a people. Exile was Judah's in-between place—in between life as they knew it and life as it was yet to be, *if* life was yet to be.

Differing perspectives emerged from this in-between place. Some exiles started to doubt Yahweh's sovereignty and began to worship Marduk, Babylon's god. Others continued to believe in Yahweh but feared that their sinfulness and disobedience had caused their alienation. However, some ("a few survivors," Isaiah 1:9) refused to view the dire circumstances as evidence of faithlessness on the part of Yahweh. This minority group boldly asserted their faith in, and commitment to, a loving, faithful God. Even though all that they knew had been destroyed, they saw their circumstances through the lens of faith, not fear. In the storm of exile, they dared to claim God's power and presence.

Exile is not limited to sixth-century B.C. Walter Brueggemann has referred to exile as "the collapse of the known world."[1] Many of us know what it is like to have life come crashing down, forever destroying the security we thought we had. What did the Flood story say to a displaced and disheartened Judah? What does it continue to say to those experiencing exile-like conditions today?

We know the story. God saw the evil of humanity and was so grieved that God decided to destroy "human beings . . . together with animals and creeping things and birds of the air, for I am sorry that I have made them" (Genesis 6:7). Because Noah was righteous and faithful, God made a covenant to spare him (6:18). Noah was faithful to God's instructions (6:22; 7:5, 16). God was faithful to God's promise to flood the earth yet save Noah and his family, who rode out the swelling waters for 150 days (7:24).

A crisis can flood our lives with change. Sometimes it trickles in, slowly eroding life as we knew it. Sometimes change comes as a torrent, jarring us from our moorings. It may even threaten without warning, like the tsunami last year, to wipe out any trace of our existence. Either way, it casts us into an in-between place. We cannot reconstruct what once was. What life will become—*if* life is to continue—lies suddenly hidden, ripped from our grasp.

In crisis, it is often only in retrospect that we see when the tide began to turn. In the Flood story, the words "but God remembered Noah" (8:1) signal the beginning of something new. Immediately, the waters subside; and God promises twice in quick succession "never again" to destroy creation (8:21). Sit up and take notice when words or phrases in Scripture are repeated, for they must be important! Then God begins the process of re-creation (9:1-17). What did God remember that inspired change? God remembered Noah's faithfulness and righteousness. That is not, however, what is emphasized at the end of the story.

The conclusion emphasizes God's covenant. After God establishes covenant with Noah in Genesis 6:18, the conclusion reemphasizes covenant, naming it seven times (9:1; 11, 12, 13, 15, 16, 17), meaning it is important! God remembered the covenant relationship with God's people. During biblical times, a covenant was a significant act. It bound two parties together through oral or written contracts, requiring them to act in particular ways. The purpose of the covenant was to establish how the parties would be in relationship. Ratification usually involved a symbolic and memorable act (15:9-10, 17-18).

The Noachic covenant is significant for several reasons. First, it is not just between two parties but between God and Noah, all of Noah's descendants, and all of creation (9:9-10). Second, this covenant requires no response; it is a gracious gift from God. Third, the covenant is eternal. What is the content of this gracious promise to all? That "never again" will God destroy creation. "Never again" is repeated, just as in 8:21, indicating that it is of extreme importance! Just to make sure we are paying attention, 9:12 again states the eternal and universal qualities of the covenant.

However, promises can sound too good to be true. We skeptical humans like more proof. True to the nature of covenants, God even offered a sign of the divine promise—"a bow in the clouds" (9:13-14, 16). Normally, a *bow* is a weapon of death and destruction used by soldiers. However, things and circumstances often take on new meaning when seen through the perspective of faith. Through the lens of covenant, what was once a sign of destruction became a sign of life. The rainbow became a tangible, visible reminder to God of the life-giving nature and loving purposes of God (9:15). Lord, give us eyes to see, too.

To those in crisis, in transition, in between life as it was and life as it will be, the Flood story offers perspective. It says though all around you may look like chaos, chaos is not the end of the story. When viewed through the lens of faith, we can see that all is under the control of our sovereign, faithful God whose purposes are for the good of creation. And we have the rainbow to prove it.

The people of exile thought they had lost everything; but when given eyes to see, they found the one thing that had been with them all along. They still had God's promise (Genesis 26:3-4; 31:3; Exodus 3:12; 4:12, 15). That means grace is sufficient to see us through the storms in life we face (2 Corinthians 12:9).

Think of a time in your life when you were in crisis or transition. Was your perspective one of fear or faith?

Was there a turning point in the event? What caused your circumstances or your perspective to change?

Where was God in the event? How did the event affect your faith? How did your perspective affect the circumstances?

A LOOK AT SUFFERING
1 Peter 3:18-22

In that ice storm two years ago, the circumstances were not the same for everybody. Our side of the block was dark and cold for five long days and nights, while the houses directly across the street were ablaze with light. While my family was huddling in front of the fireplace, eating dry cereal, and reading with flashlights, our neighbors were basking in warmth, eating hot meals, and relaxing in front of the TV. At best, our neighbors' good fortune inspired our electrical hopes. At worst, their power fueled our resentment. We were sharing the same community but experiencing it differently. Our home no longer felt like home, yet we had nowhere else to go.

Peter addressed this sense of exile and alienation (2:11) in his letter to church communities in the heart of the Roman Empire (1:1). Though the letter claims authorship by "Peter, an apostle of Jesus Christ" (1:1), it is likely that it was written in the last quarter of the first century, after Rome's capture of Jerusalem and the destruction of the Jewish Temple in A.D. 70.

A key reason why followers of Jesus were at odds with Roman society is because 40 years before, Roman soldiers had crucified their leader. The letter writer's true feelings about Rome are made evident at the end of the letter when Rome is associated with Babylon (5:13). Babylon, as we know, was the imperial force that exiled Judah (589–39 B.C.). Rome is was now the new Babylon, a thought that is echoed six times in the Book of Revelation. Rome's oppressive ideology[2] caused followers of Jesus, whose belief system was fundamentally different from that of Rome, to feel like exiles in their own land.

Life in the Roman Empire could differ greatly depending on one's circumstances. The haves had one experience; the have-nots had another. In the empire, 95 percent of the people were have-nots, First Peter's communities among them. Rome's unjust economic system did not provide the majority of the population the basics of food, clean water, and shelter. Rome's unjust use of power fueled the resentments of the have-nots.

It is likely that First Peter's audience felt alienated from Roman society because of their fundamentally different perspectives. The Roman Empire claimed that the Empire, and the emperor in particular, were agents of the gods (*their* gods, not the God of Israel). Naturally, Roman citizens were to honor the emperor (2:17) through whom all blessing would come (blessing occurring mostly for the five percent elite). A minority community that believed in the sovereignty of God manifest in the power of Christ was thus at odds with the imperial forces that asserted Rome's sovereignty.

Besides ideology, lifestyle was another differentiating factor. The Gentile recipients of the let-ter once shared the pagan beliefs of their neighbors (4:5) but now focused on righteous living (Chapters 1–2). Holy living does not always make one the most popular person at parties. A pastor friend told me he dreads the cocktail party question, "What do you do?" Inevitably, his answer causes his conversational partners to look uncomfortably at their drinks or to defend their sporadic or even non-existent church attendance. The first-century converts' change of heart probably made them feel like exiles in their own home communities.

The converts' lifestyle was no longer compatible with that of their neighbors because their priorities had changed. I can relate. I work full-time as a greeting card writer on a staff of talented, sociable writers. The other writers often get together on evenings and weekends, as did I before having kids and going to seminary. However, my faith-inspired commitments to earning a seminary degree, to working in the church, to writing on Scripture and faith, and to mothering my sons allows little time to socialize with coworkers. What I do on the outside is determined by whom God has shaped me to be on the inside. My commitment to God determines the choices I make daily.

Another possibility is that the communities to whom Peter wrote felt like aliens because they *were* aliens. John Elliott argues that many in these early Christian communities were resident aliens who had moved recently to the urban setting of Rome for gainful employment or for other reasons.[3]

A more spiritual explanation for their alienation is that Christians long for home until they reside eternally with God. As Augustine said, "Our hearts are restless until they rest in thee." It is likely that a combination of reasons contributed to the communities' sense of exile. It is not easy to be an outsider.

It is this sense of alienation and exile what we people of faith experience that the pastoral letter of First Peter addresses. After Peter's greeting to and blessing of the community of faith (1:1-12), he affirms the goodness of a life set apart to participate in God's good purposes (1:13–2:3). The covenant community of Christ's holy church (2:4-10) exists not for its own purposes but to be in ministry to the world (2:11–4:11).

What happens when the church exists within a culture whose purposes are not consistent with God's life-giving, loving, liberating purposes? First Peter gives us the news straight: To truly be the church in a world that is contrary to God's purposes is to invite suffering (1:6, 11; 2:19-23; 3:14, 17). However, contrary to what our culture teaches us, suffering is not necessarily the penalty for having done something wrong. In fact, it may just be the proof we need that we are becoming holy.

"For Christ also suffered" begins our second passage (3:18-22);
but, as we know, Christ's suffering is not the end of the story. The cross, meant for harm, was ultimately used by God for good. In Christ's journey from life to death to resurrection, God's life-giving, loving, liberating purposes are made manifest. Because God has triumphed over death, we have nothing to fear (verse 14). God's grace extends to everyone—even "spirits in prison, who in former times did not obey" (verse 19). God's grace extends not only o those marginalized in life but even those marginalized in death! Notice that the text does not name a specific form of imprisonment. We can be imprisoned in many ways—by poverty, addiction, depression, illness, and injustice, to name a few. There are those justly and unjustly incarcerated in prison as well. Jesus comes to these places of exclusion to bring all outcasts back to God.

How, then, are we brought back to God? How are we saved? Peter's simple answer is "through water," that instrument of grace that Noah first experienced. "Baptism now saves you [all]" (The Greek word for "you" is plural [verse 21].). Baptismal water does not just change us on the outside as if removing dirt. It cleanses our insides so that our "promise to God is made of a good conscience" (My translation from the Greek. "Appeal" in the New Revised Standard Version is more accurately a "promise" or "pledge.") We begin to see differently because we have become different. We are given an inner disposition that is attuned to God, which makes our outer acts holy. Indeed, our clear conscience stems from our "good conduct in Christ" (verse 16). To be sure, Noah's story teaches us that good behavior alone does not save; we need God's intervention in our lives. Water alone, in other words, does not save us. Our salvation is the result of "the resurrection of Jesus Christ" (verse 21).

God's life-giving, loving, liberating purposes were demonstrated through Jesus' life, death, and resurrection. The resurrection of Jesus and Jesus' ascent to the place of power he shares with God show that God has triumphed over suffering and death. That Jesus sits at "the right hand of God, with angels, authorities, and powers made subject to him" (verse 22) is further proof that we have nothing to fear.

Still, it can be a scary world. Until our final homecoming, we shall all live in a sort of exile—between Christ's resurrection and the final resurrection when God's good purposes are complete. A faithful life in this in-between time is difficult, but it helps when we can keep the challenges we face in perspective. Because of the Resurrection, we know the end of the story. We know where our ultimate home will be. More than that, we know that every difficulty, challenge, or adversity we face has been overcome by the power of God. As we look at life through the lens of the Resurrection, we can view everything—even suffering—in the light of divine hope.

Have you ever felt like an outsider because of your faith?

What gives you strength to persist in a holy lifestyle in the face of adversity?

How does the awareness of your baptism affect the promises you make to God?

How does the truth of the Resurrection give you hope in your daily life?

A KINGDOM PERSPECTIVE
Mark 1:9-15

Having suffered through one ice storm in which life as I knew it came crashing down, I tried to think positively that, surely, it would not happen again. I went about the day's tasks, flashlight in tow just in case. Mid-afternoon, I sat working at my desk as my sons came in for cocoa after "skating" on the driveway. I was sprinkling on marshmallows when I heard an ominous rustle, a shattering crack, and what sounded like a gunshot. The kids ran up from the basement and, wide-eyed with worry, we walked together towards the front of the house. I opened the front door to see a mass of crystallized limbs crashed against the storm door, blocking any view of the front yard. With the door pinned shut, we had to go out the back door to see the full extent of the damage. A massive tree lay across our front yard, its branches resting on the roof, our gutters dislodged and distorted. "Are we being hazed?" my high school son asked.

Though I could understand why my son felt we were being picked on by God, I assured him that according to God's covenant promises, that is not how God operates. God is actively working on God's purposes for the good for all creation. Sometimes it just does not feel like it, especially when it is cold and dark because your power lines have been ripped down yet again.

The community that Mark's Gospel addressed knew what it was to experience a deja vu of tragedy. Just as Judah had suffered under Babylonian occupation, first-century Jewish Christians suffered under the harsh social and economic conditions of Roman rule (as elaborated in the section on First Peter). Just as Babylon had captured Jerusalem and destroyed the Temple in 587 B.C., Rome captured Jerusalem (A.D. 66-70) and destroyed the reconstructed Temple in A.D. 70. Mark was composed during this time of crisis (A.D. 69-70), possibly in Rome itself. As it was for Judah in exile, so it was for the Jewish followers of Jesus in the Roman Empire.[4] Given Rome's military might and its destruction of the Temple, it seemed clear that Rome's gods had trumped the God of the one whom Rome had crucified 40 years earlier.

Once again, it is a matter of perspective. Mark's community knew that crucifixion was not the end of the story. They knew the life-giving, loving, liberating power of God demonstrated by Christ's resurrection. However, the harsh reality of daily living and the reality of defeat in the Roman Empire seemed anything but life-giving. Suffering was wearing down Mark's community, so Mark's Gospel encouraged this hard-pressed community of believers on the margin of society to continue their faithful discipleship even in suffering, even in the midst of crisis, even in the ravages of war, even when life as they knew it was crashing down around them.

So how did Mark encourage faithfulness in Jesus' followers when Rome was causing their lives to come crashing down around them? Mark began with "the good news of Jesus Christ, the Son of God." In the first century, the Greek word for "good news" was used mainly to report successful military victory. The first line in Mark boldly asserts that circumstances are not as they appear. The embers of war may still be burning, but the battle has already been won—and the winner is not Rome. The good news (the victor) is Jesus Christ, Son of God. Mark's audience may have been skeptical about God's victory, for there seemed to be plenty of evidence to the contrary; but it was all a matter of perspective.

Turns out, it depends on where you are looking. If you are looking solely at power, it might appear that there were clear winners and losers; but that was not the whole story. Mark turns our eyes away from the power center to the wilderness—first to the wilderness of Isaiah (Isaiah 40:3; Mark 1:2), then to the wilderness where John (who was *not* wearing a power suit!) was baptizing (Mark 1:2-8). Even Jesus left Galilee for the wilderness where he was baptized by John (verses 7-9). Clearly something important was taking place in the wilderness.

In biblical times, the wilderness had several connotations. Wilderness evoked Israel's exodus from Pharaoh's oppressive rule as well as Judah's exile after its defeat at the hands of Babylon. It referred to places on the fringes of society where the non-elite, the peasants, the "nobodies" resided. Wilderness was—and is—an in-between place, in between where God's people have unjustly been and where God desires God's creation to be.

The good news is that God is ever present in the wilderness. In the gnarled entanglements of the wilderness, it is not easy to keep perspective. Mark asserts that in the wilderness, in the places you may least expect it, God's acts of transformation and liberation are already underway. (This was good news for my sons and me as our front yard again became an icy wilderness.)

The passage continues with Jesus being baptized (where else?) in the wilderness (verse 9). Water, the instrument of salvation for Noah and for the communities in First Peter, played an important role in revealing Jesus' identity in Mark. As Jesus was baptized, "the heavens [were] torn apart and the Spirit descend[ed] like a dove on him" (verse 10). Just as the dove brought the sign of new life to Noah (Genesis 8:12), the dove's descent on Jesus signified the new life that Jesus would initiate. The divine voice that only Jesus could hear gave additional affirmation and instruction, beginning with "You are my Son" (Mark 1:11; 1:1). The words evoked Psalm 2:7 in which the king is called God's son, anointed or commissioned for a special purpose. What was Jesus commissioned to do?

Jesus' marching orders cast him (Mark 1:10) "immediately" into the wilderness where he would return often in the Gospel (1:35; 45; 6:31, 32, 35; 8:4). Remember: If it is repeated, it is important. Just as 40 was a significant number in the Flood story and the Exodus story, Jesus was in the wilderness for 40 days. It is as if Mark were telling us that this was not anything new. We have been in the wilderness before, and God assisted us. Rest assured: God will assist us now. In the wilderness, God assisted Jesus through the angels. Neither Satan nor the "wild beasts" were much of a threat. We are not surprised because Mark's beginning reveals the end of the story: God through Jesus has already won the battle.

Still, there would be challenges along the way. John, for instance, was arrested (1:14a). Though Jesus was victorious in the wilderness, an ominous threat clouded the horizon. In this dangerous context, Jesus proclaimed "the good news of God" (verse 14b). When the going gets tough, the tough get going in ministry. What was it, then, that Jesus, Son of God, was commissioned to do?

Jesus proclaimed that "the kingdom [or empire] of God has come near." (The Greek word for "kingdom" is also translated as "empire" or "realm" [Mark 1:15].) In the middle of the Roman Empire, at the end of the war (which Rome won!), Mark's Gospel had the audacity to proclaim that God's empire, not Rome's empire, was at hand! "Repent, and believe in the good news."

Mark's good news began by giving us the end of the story. God, through Jesus Christ, won the battle. Though there appeared to be chaos, though it appeared that the Roman Empire was in control, God was still sovereign over God's creation, with which God is in covenant relationship. Our faith assures us there is nothing to fear.

In this in-between time—between the resurrection of Christ and the time when God brings God's kingdom or empire into its fullness—we can watch and pray for God's power, knowing that God's power is enough to get us through any storm we may face.

How does the good news of God affect you in your present circumstances?

What does it mean for you to know that you are God's beloved child in whom God is "well pleased"?

In what ways do you encounter the kingdom or empire of God in your daily life?

In what ways is God calling you to participate more fully in God's purposes?

---

[1] From Interpretation: A Bible Commentary for Teaching and Preaching: *Genesis*, by Walter Brueggemann (John Knox Press, 1982); page 87.

[2] From "Roman Imperial Theology," in *Matthew and Empire: Initial Explorations*, by Warren Carter (Trinity Press International, 2001); pages 20-34.

[3] From *A Home for the Homeless: A Sociological Exegesis of 1 Peter, Its Situation and Strategy*, by John H. Elliott (Fortress, 1981); *1 Peter* (Doubleday, 2000); pages 94-103.

[4] In the first century, Christianity was considered a sect of Judaism.

Seeing Ourselves as People of God's Promise

We are surrounded by promises. If we buy the right clothes, life will be stylish. If we drive the right car, life will be exhilarating. If we purchase the right technology, life will be efficient. If we get flat-screen, high-definition, surround-sound entertainment, life will be stimulating. If we pamper ourselves, life will be comfortable. If we invest wisely, we will have prosperity. If we spend more on weapons, we will have security.

Do we believe these promises? Our identity and purpose, not to mention our priorities and goals, are shaped by our responses to these societal claims. The issue is not whether the claims have merit but whether the claims are ultimate. An inherent problem with many of society's promises is that so much is determined by us. They make us the master of our lives, our world, and our future.

Scriptures for Lent: The Second Sunday
Genesis 17:1-7, 15-16
Romans 4:13-25
Mark 8:31-38

Scripture offers an alternative. God's purposes for humankind are to participate in God's life-giving, loving, liberating purposes for all of creation. As in the story of Noah (Genesis 17:7), so in the story of Abraham: God's purpose comes in the form of a promise, a divine covenant. God's purposes are for relationship with God's creation. The ways in which we respond to God's promise determine our identity and purpose—who we are and what we do. In Romans 4:13-25, Paul writes of Abraham as the paradigmatic example of one whose life was shaped by God's gracious initiative. Abraham's obedient response can inform and inspire our own response to God's promise. In Mark 8:31-38, Jesus calls us to faithfully follow the promise, even when it leads to the cross. These texts help us to watch more faithfully for evidence of God's promise in our lives and pray for ways to live into the promise.

Our response matters, not in terms of society's rewards, but in terms of God's rewards through and because of Jesus Christ. The good news is that in faithfully participating in God's purposes, we are promised a life that is not lost but is saved, healed, and brought to wholeness (Mark 8:35).

PREPOSTEROUS PROMISE
Genesis 17:1-7, 15-16

Many of society's promises seem preposterous. Eat anything and still lose weight! Thin thighs in 30 days! Get rich quick! No cost loans! When I was growing up my dad warned me, "If it sounds too good to be true, it probably is."

The story of God's covenant with Abraham (Genesis 17:1-7, 15-16) gives evidence of having been written during and after Babylonian exile. For Judah in Babylonian exile (587-39 B.C.), the question was whether Yahweh's covenantal promises to Judah for a land and a people had been too good to be true. The land that Yahweh had promised was now under enemy occupation. Was God's promise of land no longer valid? The Temple, the central place of encounter with Yahweh, had been destroyed by Babylon. Had Yahweh recanted on the promise of presence?

Many of us know what it is to face circumstances that are far different from our expectations. "It was not supposed to turn out this way," is a commonly uttered phrase. How do we reconcile a reality that does not mesh with our dreams, an outcome that pales in comparison to the promise? We may wonder what went wrong. Was the promise false? Is the promise-giver not faithful? Did we do something wrong?

God's covenant with Abraham addressed the problem of seemingly broken promises. To Yahweh's people, struggling to find reasons to be faithful in the devastation of Babylonian exile, God's promise of continuing relationship to Abraham provided reassurance that God had not abandoned them, even though all the evidence suggested the contrary.

God's covenant with Abraham continues to address the problem of seemingly broken promises for us today. Many of us know what it is like to try to reconcile the realities of the world with God's good purposes for creation. God's life-giving purposes are not always evident. Natural disasters happen. Wars destroy God's children on both sides of enemy lines. AIDS threatens to cripple Africa for generations. Unspeakable acts of violence are afflicted upon the most defenseless. Poverty, hunger, and homelessness are daily realities for countless Americans, not to mention people worldwide. The Abraham story provides reassurance that despite much evidence to the contrary, God is still committed to God's covenantal purposes. Further, God's purposes invite our faithful and obedient participation, as modeled by Abraham.

Abraham is introduced as Abram in Genesis 11:26. To those struggling with issues of sovereignty and trust, even the genealogy provides reassurance. Just as there were ten generations between Adam and Noah (5:1-32), there are exactly ten generations between Noah and Abram (11:10-26). The God who perfectly ordered creation (Chapters 1–3) continues to create in perfect order. To those in Babylonian exile, and to us today, for whom world events seem chaotic, the genealogy asserts that there is order to God's purposes.

God's call to Abram (12:1-9) consisted of God's instruction, God's promise, and Abram's response. God told Abram to leave his home in Haran: "Go from your country and your kindred and your father's house to the land that I will show you" (12:1). With the command came a promise (12:2, 3c), which Abram obeyed (12:4a). For Abram and Sarai, becoming exiles was part of God's plan. They left the way of life they knew but took with them God's promise.

The promise was momentous in its significance—for Abram and all of humanity. God, the creator of the world, promised to make Abram a great blessing "so that [he would] be a blessing" (12:2) and that "in [with or by] you [the Hebrew preposition has all these meanings] all the families of the earth shall be blessed" (12:3). God planned to make Abram instrumental in God's purposes to bless all people. Though the promise sounded too good to be true, Abram obeyed (12:4a).

As God brought Abram, Sarai, and Lot to Canaan, God gave them another promise: "To your offspring I will give this land" (12:7). What must Abram and Sarai have been thinking as they made their way to the unknown land, all their possessions in tow? Here they were—a 75-year-old man (12:4c) and a barren woman (11:30)—leaving everything they knew to follow a promise for land that was not theirs and to receive offspring they were too old and infertile to conceive. The promise seemed preposterous. Still, they followed the promise, which was repeated (13:15-16).

Circumstances made the honoring of this promise improbable. A famine sent Abram and Sarai into exile in Egypt (12:10). A military uprising caused Lot to be captured and Abram to lead men toward Lot's rescue (14:1-16). Through all this, Abram struggled to believe God's promise (15:2-3). God reiterated the promise of descendants (15:1-6) and land (15:7-21) by making a covenant with Abram (15:18). (This is the first of two accounts of God's covenant with Abram preserved in Genesis. The second is in Chapter 17.) When Sarai had still not conceived, she suggested to Abram that he bear a child with her slave girl, Hagar, which Abram did (16:1-16).

At this point, it seemed doubtful that the promise of an heir from Abram and Sarai would be fulfilled, since Abram was now 99 years old (17:1). Still, God reiterated the promise in the form of a covenant. Unlike God's covenant with Noah that did not require a response (9:1-17), God's covenant with Abram did. Abram's response resulted in identity and purpose.

Genesis 17:1 addressed God's identity: "I am God Almighty." Who Abram was had everything to do with who God is. Then God gave Abram his purpose: "Walk before me." Humanity's purpose is to be with God. The intention of a life lived in relationship to God is given in the form of a command: "Be blameless." (The Hebrew word for "blameless" could also be translated as "whole" or "complete" [17:1].)

The promise continued. Again God promised "exceedingly numerous" descendants (verse 2). Abram responded by "falling on his face," a sign of worship (verse 3). In his commissioning of Abram, God gave him a new identity and function: He will be *Abraham*, "ancestor of a multitude of nations" (verse 5). Even kings and nations would come from him

(verse 6). Not bad for a resident alien. Still the question remained: Could Abraham trust God in the midst of seemingly impossible circumstances?

Abraham could trust God because God had made a covenant with him. So important is covenant that the word is repeated four times in seven verses (verses 2, 4, 7a, 7c). Remember: Take notice when words in Scripture are repeated! The essence of God's covenant with Abraham was that God promised "to be God to you and to your offspring after you" (verse 7). For people who have lost all they have known or have hoped for, this promise assures that God is still their God. The promise sustained the people in exile. It sustains people in dire circumstances today.

In a *60 Minutes* interview, Episcopalian bishop Gene Robinson described the time in his life when it seemed like he had lost everything. At age 39, he had just gotten a divorce and told his bishop that he was gay, knowing this admission could cause severe implications for his ministry. "It was a very difficult time in my life, and I thought I might lose everything," says Robinson. "At night, I would go to bed and all I would have was my integrity and God. And what I learned from that was that it was just enough."[1]

God's covenant assures us that God will not abandon God's people, no matter the situations we encounter. The promise can be trusted, for it is an "everlasting covenant" (verse 7).

For Abraham, however, there remained the unresolved matter of *how* the promise of offspring could be fulfilled, for Sarai was still barren (11:30). For Judah, there remained the question of how God's promise could be fulfilled for them, for they felt "bereaved and barren, exiled and put away" (Isaiah 49:21). God's promise addressed these matters by changing Sarai's identity and purpose. Her name would become *Sarah*, said God; and "I will bless her, and . . . give you a son by her . . . and she shall give rise to nations; kings of people shall come from her" (Genesis 17:16).

We know the rest of the story. We know that God's preposterous promise came true. Scripture tells us it is in God's nature to do amazing things. "I am about to do a new thing; / now it springs forth, do you not perceive it?" (Isaiah 43:19). God's new things are not based on past events or present circumstances but on the nature and purposes of God. For Abraham and Isaac, the new thing was the baby Isaac (Genesis 21:1-5). For Judah in Babylonian exile, the fulfillment of God's promise was the reassurance of their identity as God's people. It reaffirmed their commitment to follow God, even when evidence of God's sovereignty was hard to see.

As it was then, so it is now. We can trust in God's promises because God is faithful. God has committed to bless all families in the earth, and God wants humanity's participation in the furthering of God's loving purposes.

The good news is that God will forever keep God's promises. What is more, God's promises will forever keep us.

How has God been present to you during a time of unfulfilled expectation?

What does God's promise "to be God to you and to your offspring after you" (Genesis 17:7) mean to you?

How does God's promise affect your priorities and sense of purpose?

RADICAL RESPONSE
Romans 4:13-25

Seemingly impossible situations can take many forms. In the Roman church that Paul was addressing, the challenge was people who could not get along because of differing views about ways to be faithful. (Unfortunately, that is still a problem for the contemporary church!)

Paul wrote his letter to the Roman church from Corinth about A.D. 57 (Acts 20:2-3). The situation in the Roman church (which Paul had neither founded nor visited [Romans 1:10; 15:22]) was similar to a situation Paul was facing in Jerusalem. The differing practices of Jewish and Gentile

Christians were causing tension within the church. Paul wrote the letter to the Romans to help them understand that Jews and Gentiles are sinners before God (1:18–3:20), and Jews and Gentiles relate to God through faith in Christ (3:21–8:39). It was Paul's hope that right thinking would lead to right action and take the form of faithful living.

Like Abraham, Paul experienced a holy encounter that gave him a new identity and purpose. Formerly, Saul was a persecutor of Christians (Acts 8:1-4) before his encounter with God that resulted in Paul's new identity and purpose (Acts 9:1-31; Galatians 1:11–2:10). He began his letter to the Romans naming who he was and what he was called to do: "Paul, a servant of Jesus Christ, called to be an apostle, set apart for the gospel of God" (Romans 1:1). His specific purpose was "to bring about the obedience of faith among all the Gentiles for the sake of [Christ's] name" (1:5).

Paul also described the identity and purpose of his audience. They were "called to belong to Jesus Christ" (1:6). A reminder of our identity can be an admonition for correct behavior. A friend from a small town in Iowa said that before he went out as a teenager, his father would say, "Remember, you are an Everett." He knew his father was also saying, "Behave accordingly." Apparently, those in the Roman church were not behaving as those who are "called to be saints" (1:7).

The problem was a disagreement over the religious practices of Jewish and Gentile Christians (14:1–15:13). Jewish Christians continued to express their faithfulness through religious practices such as eating certain foods (Daniel 1:8-16; Judith 12:1-4), honoring the sabbath (1 Maccabees 2:32-41), and circumcising men (Genesis 17:9-14), not as ways to earn God's favor but as ways to exhibit their Jewishness. Gentile Christians, believing in grace through Christ, believed such practices were unnecessary (Romans 14:1-6).

Dissension is familiar territory to me, being a parent. I am often drawn into fights between my sons. Each will passionately state his case, want my allegiance, and demand that I lay down the law to the other. On my better days, I refuse to take sides and use the occasion for a teaching opportunity, which is just what Paul did.

Instead of taking sides, Paul reminded the squabbling Jewish and Gentile Christian factions in Rome of their identity. They were "God's beloved . . . called to be saints" through the grace of our Lord Jesus Christ (1:7). Paul wanted them to think correctly. He hoped that right thinking (Chapters 1–11) would lead to right action (Chapters 12–16). Paul argued that all people (Jew and Gentile) sin (1:18–3:20), and all (Jew and Gentile) get right with God only through faith obediently lived (3:21–8:39).

In Romans 4, Paul illustrated how persons get right before God by retelling the story of Abraham. Abraham's story was familiar to Paul, as he was "advanced in Judaism" before becoming a Jewish Christian (Galatians 1:14). Paul knew that God commissioned Abram (Genesis 12) and promised Abram offspring (Genesis 15:4-5) and that Abram believed the Lord "and the LORD reckoned it to him as righteousness" (Genesis 15:6). Significant to Paul was the order of events. God named Abram righteous and promised him descendants on the basis of belief alone (Genesis 15:6). Abraham was then circumcised as a response to God's gracious covenantal initiative (Genesis 15:18; 17:1-7, 9-14). Key for Paul was that God's gift of righteousness *preceded* Abraham's circumcision. Because Abraham was reckoned righteous before he acted righteously, Abraham became the "ancestor of a multitude of nations" (17:5) on the basis of belief alone.

Paul emphasized God's promise in Romans 4:13: "For the promise that [Abraham] would inherit the world did not come to Abraham or to his descendants through the law but through the righteousness of faith." Abraham was made the ancestor of all because he believed the Lord, not because he was circumcised. The same is true for us today. It is belief that makes us descendants of Abraham.

There is also good news for Jewish Christians. If only ethnic Jews who keep the Law are Abraham's descendants, then Abraham's faith was unnecessary (verses 14-15). As Brendan Byrne has noted, "Righteousness by faith and righteousness by law [are] mutually exclusive."[2] The Law has caused us to recognize that all people are sinners (1:18–3:20). The good news for Jewish (and Gentile) Christians is that God gives righteousness through faith. Therefore, all Christians, through belief, have Abraham as their ancestor and Christ as their brother (1:16-17; 4:16-17).

Having established Abraham's identity and purpose, Paul next emphasized God's identity and purpose. The God in whom Abraham believed "gives life to the dead and calls into existence the things that do not exist" (4:17b). Abraham believed in the God of creation, the God who does "a new thing" (Isaiah 43:19); but Abraham's belief was more than just his feeling or opinion.

Abraham's belief was one of persevering hope even when all evidence of God's promises was lacking. He had the audacity to hope for new life even when his and Sarah's bodies seemed dead to the possibility of childbearing (Romans 4:18-19). Abraham's faith was not based on his potential. It was focused on God, whose life-giving promises could be trusted (verses 20-21). Unlike humanity at large (1:21), Abraham gave the glory to God. For this reason, Abraham's faith "was reckoned to him as righteousness" (4:22).

For Paul, "God's righteousness was understood as God's activity in drawing individuals into and sustaining them within the relationship, as 'the power of God for salvation.' "[3] Righteousness was a force that moved persons from one way of being to another (1:16-17). Paul wanted us to think of God in the same trusting, reliant way. He wanted us to live empowered by this kind of transformative faith.

Paul next explained how God's promise to Abraham has far-reaching implications. The righteousness reckoned to Abraham "will be reckoned to us who believe in him who raised Jesus our Lord from the dead" (4:24). In other words, all who believe in the power of the Resurrection share the faith of Abraham, who believed in the power of bringing life from the dead. To followers of Christ in the first-century Roman church and in the church today, Paul says, You are descendants of Abraham, members of a family of faith in which "there is no longer Jew or Greek, . . . slave or free, . . . male and female" (Galatians 3:28).

Since identity is closely related to purpose, Paul concluded his argument by naming God's purpose in Jesus, who was "handed over to death for our trespasses and was raised for our justification" (Romans 4:25). Here Paul alluded to the fourth Servant Song (Isaiah 53:5, 12). In the devastating circumstances of Judahite exile, the death of the servant would "make many righteous" (Isaiah 53:11). In the saving power of the Resurrection, God justified Jesus and all who belong to Jesus (Romans 4:25). Just as Abraham was blessed to be a blessing (Genesis 12:2), so also are we. Just as Abraham was instructed to "walk before [God], and be blameless (17:1), so also are we.

What would Paul say to those in the church today who find themselves on opposite sides of divisive issues?

Think of an issue you have struggled with. How does your identity and purpose as a child of Abraham and the resurrected Christ affect your thinking? How does it affect your actions?

For Paul, righteousness was a way that God empowers God's people. How have you experienced God's power in your life?

LIVING OUT OF AND INTO THE PROMISE
Mark 8:31-38

In our society, one's identity is telling. Who you are can determine the choices you make, as well as how much adversity you face in making those choices. Membership has its privileges. Those with the right name, background, income level, or charge card are afforded promises the general public is not. Our Gospel text speaks to this issue of identity, promise, and purpose and redefines what is "the good life."

At the time the Gospel According to Mark was written (circa A.D. 69-70), issues of identity and purpose were of crucial importance for Mark's audience. They were a hard-pressed community of Jewish Christians, most likely in Rome. Between A.D. 66 and 70, Rome and Judea were at war. By 69, the defeat of Jerusalem and the destruction of the Temple were inevitable. The identity of Christians as followers of Jesus, whom Rome had crucified for rebellion 40 years earlier, was in itself problematic. Their purpose, the way they lived their faith, was called into question when the Temple was destroyed.

Mark addressed these issues by discussing Jesus' identity and the response his identity generated. The Gospel reveals Jesus' identity in the first verse: "Jesus Christ, the Son of God." *Christ*, or *Messiah* (the same word in Greek), literally means "the anointed one," one who has been commissioned. At the time of the Gospel writing, "Son of God" did not necessarily refer to divinity. The Roman emperor, for example, regularly received the title, the "son of God"; and, reflecting the patriarchal structures of the time, Paul often referred to Christians as "sons of God" (which the NRSV has consistently translated as "children of God" [Romans 8:14, 19; Galatians 3:26]). In the Hebrew tradition, "son of God" was used to refer to one who was "christed" or anointed as an agent of God commissioned to carry out God's reign (Psalm 2:2, 7).

What was Jesus "christed" to do? He was commissioned to identify for us God's realm (Mark 1:15) and to reveal God's purposes (1:22; 2:10; 3:15; 6:7). He was commissioned to have authority over evil spirits (1:21-28) and diseases (1:29-31), authority to forgive sin (2:1-12); and authority over the natural world (4:35-41) and political orders (5:1-20).

Those who understood what Jesus was about were treated in Mark as "insiders," while those who responded negatively were "outsiders" (4:10-12). It is not always clear who is on the inside and who is on the outside, however. Even disciples questioned Jesus' identity (4:41) and did not understand (4:13). Sometimes, those who were supposed to be outsiders, such as Jairus, a synagogue leader, did understand (5:22-43).

Insiders and outsiders questioned the identity of Jesus (6:14-16). When Jesus was with his disciples, he asked, "Who do people say that I am?" (8:27). He then asked his disciples, "But who do you say that I am?" (verse 29). Clearly it mattered to Jesus that his disciples understood. Peter answered, "You are the Messiah" (verse 29); and Jesus told them not to tell anyone (verse 30).

The reason Jesus would not let his disciples tell that he was the Messiah was that they only saw him as a powerful representative of God, not as one who would suffer. In verse 31, Jesus revealed that true discipleship involves suffering, rejection, and even death. Peter's understanding of Jesus as Messiah did not include these bleak promises, so he rebuked Jesus (verse 32). Jesus, in turn, rebuked Peter, saying, "Get behind me, Satan! For you are setting your mind not on divine things but on human things" (verse 33). Jesus rebuked Peter for still thinking as an outsider.

Jesus was commissioned to proclaim the good news of the realm of God in our midst (1:15). The promises of God's kingdom are not the same as the promises of society, which, for Mark's Gospel, was the Roman Empire. Jesus then explained the membership requirements for God's kingdom to the crowd and the disciples: "If any want to become my followers, let them deny themselves and take up their cross and follow me" (8:34). Membership is open to anyone. Read the small print before signing, though, Jesus said. Know what is being promised.

For Jesus, the promise included the cross. The cross was the tortuous instrument used "as a means of execution employed for foreigners or provincials who were judged to have rebelled against Rome's empire."[4] Followers of Jesus are to follow the crucified one. Membership involves a different set of rules than those of society, Jesus explained. "Those who want to save their life will lose it, and those who lose their life for my sake, and for the sake of the gospel, will save it" (verse 35). Those who place themselves outside of God's promises will be outside the rewards of God's kingdom (verses 36-38).

Who would sign up for such an offer? Why would anyone in the first century want to follow one who was going to the cross? Why would anyone follow today when society promises lives that are stylish, exhilarating, efficient, stimulating, comfortable, autonomous, prosperous, and secure?

God promises that if we claim our identity as ones shaped by the power and suffering of Christ, we can watch and pray for faithful ways to participate in the "new things" God is doing. We will encounter the power of the risen Christ and be transformed into who God has created us to be. We may not have a life rich in all that society promises, but we will have a life that is brought to wholeness through Christ (verse 35). God has promised.

In what ways have you or your community encountered the power of Christ though acts of service or suffering?

In what ways has God commissioned you or your community to be God's representative?

How does prayer help you to persist in faithful discipleship?

---

[1]From "Being Honest" at *http://www. cbsnews.com/stories/2004/03/04/60minutes/m ain604060.shtml*

[2]From *Romans*, by Brendan Byrne, ed. Daniel J. Harrington, Sacra Pagina Series, Vol. 6 (Liturgical Press, 1996); page 152.

[3]From *The Theology of Paul the Apostle*, by James G. D. Dunn (William B. Eerdmans Publishing Company, 1998); page 344.

[4]From *Pontius Pilate: Portraits of a Roman Governor*, by Warren Carter (Liturgical Press, 2003); page 57.

Seeing a New Way to Live

Scriptures for Lent: The Third Sunday

Exodus 20:1-17
1 Corinthians 1:18-25
John 2:13-22

A friend of mine works for a large corporation that is merging with another large corporation. The deals have been made. The pictures of hand-shaking CEOs have been in the paper. Now comes the painstaking process of combining two organizations into one. My friend does not know if or in what city she will have a job in the new structure. The only thing certain is that life will be different. She is living with the question of how she will now live.

Many situations—job change or loss, illness, divorce, the effects of aging, a child leaving or returning home, a family member who requires care, the death of a loved one, the impact of a natural disaster—can dramatically alter the way in which we live. Significant change can cause us to ask, How now will we live?

Questions of power or authority can come into play. How could this happen? we may ask, questioning the authority of the one who caused the change. Often, change is caused by, or results in, a change in power. My friend does not know whether the woman for whom she has worked for over a decade will continue to be her boss. A colleague, fearing her aging parents are not caring well enough for themselves, turned to the legal system to see if she has the power to intervene (the answer was no). Often parents and grandparents bemoan the lack of power they have over their grown children or grandchildren's lives. Change happens; and, often, change brings challenge.

Our Lenten texts in this chapter address changing circumstances and questions emerge. How now shall we live? Who has power? In whom do we place our trust? Exodus 20:1-17 addresses the way sixth-century Judah was to live as people of faith in Yahweh in the aftermath of the Babylonian conquering of Jerusalem and the destruction of the Temple (587 B.C.). First Corin-thians 1:18-25 addresses issues of power and allegiance for Jewish and Gentile Christians trying to merge their beliefs and lifestyle in the context of the Roman Empire. John 2:13-22 addresses issues of power, authority, and lifestyle as John's community struggled to find a way to live in the Roman Empire in the aftermath of Rome's destruction of the Temple (A.D. 70). As we examine these texts, let us examine our own hearts and lives, asking to what powers we give allegiance. Let us pray for faithful ways to live into God's life-giving, liberating purposes.

THROUGH THE LENSES OF GOD'S GRACIOUS LAW
Exodus 20:1-17

As my friend wonders who her new boss will be, my sons and I are dealing with issues of authority. "You are not the boss of me," my 11-year-old Timmy said to me as I was trying to teach him and his older brother the fine art of doing laundry. As my sons begin to stand taller and become physically stronger than I am, the question of authority has surfaced—especially at chore time. "Actually, Timmy," I explained, "At this point in our lives, I *am* the boss of you. And I expect you to contribute to our household—for our good, for your good. Now, start folding."

In and after exile in the sixth-century B.C., when it is believed our present version of Exodus was written, the question of

how to live in changing circumstances was crucial for Judah. They were a community fragmented by location, by questions of faith, by ideas on how to live. Their world had been shattered with the capture of Jerusalem and the destruction of the Temple (587 B.C.). With no Temple and no home, how could they encounter God's presence, receive atonement, and know God's will? In the Babylonian empire, which asserted sovereignty and demanded allegiance, whose power would be ultimate—that of Marduk the Babylonian god or Yahweh?

The good news of Exodus is Yahweh's power to liberate God's people from powers that oppose God's purposes. We know the story: Exodus begins with a conflict between the Lord and Pharaoh over who has power over Israel (1:1–15:21). The Lord, sovereign over nature, attacked Pharaoh with plagues (Chapters 7–10). When Pharaoh refused to give up his oppressive practices that made slaves of Israel, tragically, first-born Egyptian males and animals were slain (Chapters 11–12). Pharaoh continued to oppose the Lord's purposes and chased the fleeing Israelites to the Red Sea (Chapter 13). Demonstrating ultimate power, the Lord destroyed Pharaoh's army while delivering Yahweh's people from the powers of oppression and death.

God commissioned Moses to be the agent of God's liberating, life-giving power (3:1–4:30; 6:2–7:7). From the Red Sea, Yahweh's people "went into the wilderness" (15:22)—an in-between place—in between what they once knew (Pharaoh's oppressive rule) and the Promised Land that was yet to be (12:25).

As Yahweh's people struggled to find new ways to live, God continued to demonstrate God's sovereign power and reassuring presence. God provided water (15:22-27), manna (Chapter 16), and a structure for worship and governance (Chapter 18). God's presence was revealed in God's revelation of covenantal law in which the Ten Commandments were given to Israel (20:1-17).

The Law is a key aspect of God's covenantal promises to God's people. Note, however, that the Law is given 20 chapters into Exodus. Jewish theology begins with God's grace. Grace comes in the form of election, covenant, deliverance, and only then, law.

The role of the Law in God's covenant has been given the name "Covenantal Nomism" by scholar E. P. Sanders.[1] The term addresses the aspects of "getting in" and "staying in" God's covenant. As Sanders explains,

In the common Jewish view, God graciously chose Israel and gave them his law; that they were to obey it; that transgression was punished and obedience rewarded; that God's grace modified punishment in several ways, since God wished not to condemn and destroy; that he displayed mercy so as to lead people to repentance; that they could repent and atone; that God could also effect atonement by punishing those who were basically loyal to him; that obedience and atonement kept people in the covenant of grace.[1]

At the heart of God's covenant with Israel was grace. In grace, God elected Israel to participate in God's covenant. God's people were given a way to respond to God's grace. In direct address, God gave the Ten Commandments to the Israelites (Exodus 20:1-17; Deuteronomy 5:6-21). Yahweh's people, who had neither land nor temple in which to live out God's covenantal commitments, were given the gift of the Law. Their obedient response to God's gracious initiative would define who they were as a people.

After God emphasized God's holiness, Moses ascended Mount Sinai for the third time to receive God's words for God's people (Chapter 19). The Decalogue begins with God's direct address (20:1). God began by stating God's identity and purpose: "I am the LORD your God, who brought you out of the land of Egypt, out of the house of slavery" (verse 2). Who Israel was, as a people, was first and foremost defined by who God was. God said, "I am Yahweh"—the same name emphasized throughout the story of Exodus (3:15-16; 7:5). God's purposes are integral to God's identity: God liberates from powers that oppose God's purposes.

God is sovereign, all-powerful, and liberating. That established, the first command was given: "You shall have no other gods before me" (20:3). It is a command that can also be translated as "there shall be for you no other gods." The imperative is then an indicative, an exclamation of sovereign freedom from all competing claims by other gods to possess Israel. Being enslaved by forces that oppose God's purposes affects all areas of life: social, political, economic, and religious. The Exodus showed that God delivered people from the grasp of oppressive powers. Accordingly, God's people knew that this God could be trusted. This God was worthy of one's complete allegiance—even and especially when it appeared that oppressive empires had control. This was good news for Judah in Babylonian exile, living amidst competing claims of sovereignty. This is good news for us, living amidst the social, political, economic, and religious forces that appear to determine our fate. Aligning ourselves with God, the ultimate power, is a life-giving, liberating choice.

The second command reveals more about the God to whom all allegiance should be given (verses 4-6). God is a "jealous God" who desires ultimate allegiance (verse 5). One cannot serve two masters (Matthew 6:24; Luke 16:13). The command reveals the required response in the form of a three-fold negative: "You shall not make ... bow down to ... or worship" an idol (Exodus 20:4-6). Walter Brueggemann argues that to make God into an idol or an image, "a visible representation of Yahweh," is "an attempt to locate Yahweh and so diminish something of Yahweh's terrible freedom."[2] To align oneself with God is to accept that God is who God is (verse 1), not who we would like God to be. We are to participate in God's purposes; we do not enlist God to participate in our purposes.

Those who do not align with and participate in God's power and purposes will be punished for generations (verse 5), whereas those who do participate in God's purposes will be rewarded with "steadfast love" (verse 6). Consistent with God's nature and purposes, punishment is limited (three to four generations) while divine reward remains eternal (the thousandth generation). In other words, God rewards faithfulness and punishes disobedience. As Judah considered the devastation of their circumstances, they saw that God had been faithful to God's covenantal commitments. It was God's people who had been disobedient. Yahweh was still in charge. They were to live in faithful obedience.

The third command concerns the use of God's sovereign name. To invoke the name of Yahweh is to manifest God's power and presence. To do so towards an end that is contrary to God's purposes is to attempt to use God for one's own purpose. One who tries to use or domesticate God for one's own purposes, "the LORD will not acquit" (verse 7).

Having addressed God's sovereignty, God's freedom, and God's holy name, the fourth commandment concerns God's holy time: "Remember the sabbath day and keep it holy" (verse 8). The next verses elaborate, acknowledging the importance of work (verse 9) and the importance of refraining from work (verse 10). This command extends to all people, even animals—"you, your son or your daughter, your male or female slave, your livestock, or the alien resident in your towns" (verse 10).

Life under the oppressive rule of empires—Pharaoh's, Babylon's, or empires of present-day—has ways of living that benefit the elite at the expense of the rest. Life in God's empire is different. God's law blesses and includes as equal all whom empires marginalize— women, slaves, young people, foreigners, and exiles. The reason all are blessed is explained in verse 11: How we live has everything to do with the One who created us. The LORD created the world and rested. God is our reason and model for being. God's purposes are to be our purposes, which will result in the flourishing of all creation.

What good news this is! We, like the Judeans in exile, may look at our circumstances and feel out of control. We may feel that those who have power over our jobs, our living circumstances, our politics, or our financial situation are

determining our fate. The Ten Commandments declare that God, who created the cosmos, is, has been, and always shall be in control. No matter who seems to have power, God has ultimate power; and God uses God's power for the flourishing of all creation.

The next six commandments address the question of how God's people are to live if the laws and priorities of prevailing empires are not ultimate. How does one survive as an exile in surroundings that are less than life-giving? God gives an alternative code by which to live: a way of life that honors God and the rest of creation. For example, God says to "honor your father and mother" (verse 12), not to murder (verse 13), not to commit adultery (verse 14), not to steal (verse 15), and not to bear false witness against (verse 16) or covet anything belonging to a neighbor (verse 17). God's people are to live in right relationship with God and one another, valuing and contributing to the flourishing of all creation.

The good news of Exodus to all who are imprisoned by structures or situations that are not life-giving and loving is that God offers an alternative. In God's empire, mutual flourishing is the goal. To align with God's power, presence, and purposes is to watch and pray for ways to live in relation to God and one another.

What do you believe God's purposes are for the flourishing of your life? your family? your community?

How could you more fully live into God's purposes?

In what ways do you feel you are living in right relationship with God and with creation?

THROUGH DIFFERENCES
1 Corinthians 1:18-25

Believers in Corinth in the mid-50s were dealing with questions of lifestyle and power. Paul, who founded the church in Corinth three years earlier (Acts 18) was made aware of these struggles through visits (1 Corinthians 1:11; 5:1; 16:17-18) and letters (7:1) from church members.

The first issue concerned how these followers of Christ were to live. The problem was that believers were merging the "now and the not yet," claiming to be sharing already in the fullness of God's rule that is yet to be (4:8-10). Additionally, they were separating what should have been joined: their spiritual beliefs and their outward actions. They were not living in right relationship with God and one another, as evidenced by reports on immorality (5:1); lawsuits against one another (6:1); marriage, sex, and spirituality (7:1-40); and food and idolatry (Chapters 8–10).

A second issue concerned power. It appears that different factions were emerging within the community as members gave their allegiance to different spiritual leaders (1:11-12). They seem to have been asserting superiority, as manifested by their "boasting" (verse 29) and "puffed-up" behavior (4:6). Thankfully for the church, questions of how to live a Christian life and issues of power have been successfully resolved; and those quarrels are a matter of ancient history. Right? If only!

In the church today, divisions still abound. There are faithful people on both sides of almost every controversial issue. When the media reports on the church, the story is often about differing positions over gay marriage, abortion, evolution in schools, whether or not women or practicing homosexuals should be ordained. The story is often about tragic abuses of power as in cases of clergy sex abuse of children. We also hear about the misappropriation of church funds. If only the dominant story the media told about the church were the ways in which we are addressing injustice, poverty, hunger, the global AIDS crisis, or tsunami relief!

Differences and divisions are a reality in the church. The church is comprised of people who are dependent on the power and grace of our Creator God. Although broken, the church is called to manifest God's power and presence, to participate faithfully in God's purposes. What does Paul say to the church mired in struggle in Corinth? What does Paul say to the church today? How, now, shall we live?

First, Paul addresses the question of who is in charge. He begins the letter establishing his authority, saying he is "called to be an apostle of Christ Jesus by the will of God" (1:1). It is because of who God and Jesus are that Paul is who he is, doing what he is doing. God, through Christ, is the boss of him. That being established, Paul names the problem of factions caused by diverging allegiances (verses 10-12) and implores them to remember the reason they exist as a church: the good news of the cross of Christ (verse 17).

In the middle of the first century, a cross in the Roman Empire was not good news. A cross was an instrument of torture that the Roman Empire used to cause a slow, painful, and public death for those who defied Rome's purposes. It served to shock, horrify, and warn all bystanders against insurgent ideas.

A ghastly contemporary parallel would be the horrific images from Iraq that captors produced and distributed that show them standing with beheading weapons over a kneeling hostage. The horror of it is unspeakable. Imagine the decapitation instrument being labeled "good news."

In the Roman Empire in the first century, beheading was the least severe form of death. Decapitation was reserved for Roman citizens. Increasing in severity was being burned to death. The "most wretched of deaths," as historian Josephus described (*JW* 7.203), was crucifixion. Crucifixion demonstrated the power of the Roman Empire over anyone who dared to oppose it.

Yet Paul called the cross "good news" (verse 17) and elaborated his reasoning in verses 18-25. Paul could call the cross good news because it was proof positive that the power of Rome was no match for the greater power of God. Rome tried to "shock and awe" followers of Christ by demonstrating the power of the cross to kill; but the cross was not the end of the story, as Paul knew. We, too, know the power of resurrection.

Paul spent eight verses saying, "Friends, things are not as they seem. Those who think they are so smart really are not that smart in the realm where it really counts— God's empire. Those who think they have power are powerless if they are not aligned with God's purposes."

The good news? "Christ crucified . . . to those who are the called . . . [is] the power of God" (verses 23-24). Clearly, Paul was talking about a different kind of power than Rome's power. To Paul, the power of God was the good news of Christ. It was "the power of God for salvation" (Romans 1:16). The Greek word for *power* is *dunamis*— the root of our word for *dynamite*. God powers us into salvation, into being healed whole with force. The power of the gospel can take us, with explosive force, from one way of living to another, from one set of priorities to a more life-giving way, from structures that oppress and marginalize to a way to flourish.

In addition to power, Paul proclaimed that "Christ crucified ... to those who are the called ... [is] the wisdom of God" (1:23, 24). Clearly, God's wisdom is different from "the wisdom of the world" (1 Corinthians 1:20). The sweep of Scripture reveals that God's wisdom gives life (Proverbs 8:25; Baruch 4:1) by providing shelter (Proverbs 9:1), abundant food and drink (Proverbs 9:5; Sirach 24:21), and the gift of God's law (Sirach 15:1-3; 19:20; 24:23).

So, who are "the called" who participate in God's power and wisdom? Paul says that those who are called are "both Jews and Greeks." In other words, everyone. In today's language, "the called" would be liberals and conservatives, haves and haves-nots, two-thirds world and one-third world. God's purposes are for all God's creation to flourish.

Good news for all could sound too good to be true. How can we trust this news when we are caught in situations that seem to be anything but good news?

Paul said that we can trust this news, because even in our foolishness "God decided to save those who believe" (1 Corinthians 1:21). It all comes down to God's grace. However, it does not end with grace. There is the matter of our response—how we are to live.

Paul said God saves those who believe (verse 21). For Paul, to believe was to live in faithful obedience, participating in God's good purposes, as did Abraham. It is not an easy job, but it is a profession that leads to life. As long as we remember who is Boss.

Think of an area of struggle in your life. How does your participation in God's power inform and impact this struggle?

How does God's wisdom inform and affect areas of struggle in the church today?

What might Paul say to the divisions in the church today?

THROUGH ADVERSITY
John 2:13-22

Power was at issue for John's community in the 80s A.D. Only a decade prior, Rome had sacked Jerusalem and decimated the Temple. John's community, a marginalized group of mainly Jewish followers of Jesus living in the Roman Empire, would appear to have no power in their present circumstances. The Temple had been for these Jewish Christians a place of significance in which God's presence was experienced, God's will was encountered, and God's forgiveness was received. With its destruction came the pressing question, How, now, shall we live? There was also a question of power. Whose power was greater—Rome's or God's?

John's Gospel clearly addresses the authority of Jesus, the Word made flesh (1:1-14). Jesus was sent by God (5:24; 6:57; 8:29). We know that God was the boss of Jesus because Jesus did God's will (5:19; 8:29), performed God's works (5:36), and spoke God's words (8:40; 14:10, 24).

In John, one of the earliest works Jesus performed was to attack the unjust practices that the Temple was perpetuating (2:13-23).[4] In the passage that precedes this text, Jesus manifested God's power and presence by changing water to wine at the wedding in Cana (verses 1-11). He then went to Capernaum, a place away from the power center of Jerusalem, with his mother, brothers, and disciples (verse 12).

Our Lenten text sets the scene: "The Passover of the Jews was near, and Jesus went up to Jerusalem." The Passover setting evokes the first Passover in Exodus in which God delivered God's people (Exodus 12:1-28). We are reminded that God, who sent Jesus, is a God who liberates from oppressive powers. Jesus was going up to Jerusalem, a place in which the political/religious elite wielded their power.

In biblical times, there was no distinction between the social, political, religious, and economic spheres. The Temple, though of profound religious significance for Jews, was also the primary political institution of Jerusalem and served as the bank for Jerusalem's elite. The practices of the five percent elite who taxed their tenants up to 70 percent of their yields were carried out through the Temple system. The Temple was at the heart of an exploitative and oppressive system that was anything but life-giving to the majority of the people (Jeremiah 7).

So what did Jesus do upon surveying the Temple economy? (2:14). "Making a whip of cords, he drove all of them out of the temple, both the sheep and the cattle. He also poured out the coins of the moneychangers and overturned their tables. He told those who were selling the doves, 'Take these things out of here! Stop making my Father's house a marketplace!'" (verses 15-16). Jesus, who was sent by God, who did the works of God and said the words of God, opposed structures and systems that oppose God's life-giving, liberating purposes.

Following Jesus' actions, "his disciples remembered that it was written, 'Zeal for your house will consume me'" (verse 17). Psalm 69 is a prayer for deliverance from persecution. God is a god who delivers God's people from powers that are contrary to God's purposes, but questions abounded. The Jews asked, "What sign can you show us for doing this?" (John 2:18). In the midst of change, we want to know if the one in charge can be trusted.

Jesus answered, "Destroy this temple, and in three days I will raise it up" (verse 19). A seemingly preposterous answer! The Jews responded, "This temple has been under construction for forty-six years, and you will raise it up in three days?" (verse 20). The text goes on to interpret: "But he was speaking of the temple of his body" (verse 21). Jesus would become the new temple after he was "lifted up" (3:14; 8:28; 12:32, 34).

Here we have an amazing reversal of power! For John's community, struggling with life under Roman rule, enduring the loss of the Temple, trying to figure out who had the power and how they were to live, the gospel interprets history through the lens of belief. The gospel says that things are not as they seem. Rome thought it had the power. Rome sacked Jerusalem and destroyed the Temple; but, said John, what Rome meant for harm, God used for good. The new locus of God's power and presence—the new place in which God's presence is encountered, God's will is known, and God's forgiveness is received is in Jesus.

The passage concludes, "After he was raised from the dead, his disciples remembered that he had said this; and they believed the scripture and the word that Jesus had spoken" (verse 22). We can trust this good news. God raised Jesus from the dead. God conquered death, which shows that God's power is greater than any power this earth can bring. By believing—by living in right relationship with God and with creation—we participate in God's purposes for creation.

As I was completing this Lenten study, I received an e-mail from my friend updating me about the merger situation. All is still uncertain, she said. Yesterday was, like most work days, crisis-filled, anxiety-ridden, and deadline-driven. It had a different ending than most, though. My friend's boss came by to tell her how much she valued her positive, reassuring presence. My friend's kindness and care for her boss has made all the difference in her boss's sanity these past weeks. The corporation has its own agenda, priorities, and pace; but my friend has chosen to abide by a different set of priorities. She knows who her boss is.

Think of structures or situations that have power in your life. How do God's purposes for the flourishing of all creation critique such powers?

Think of those who are marginalized in our society or enslaved by powers of racism, poverty, xenophobia, or addiction. In what ways can these people experience God's purposes for flourishing?

In what ways, big or small, are you being called to participate in God's purposes of liberating from powers that oppress?

---

[1]From *Judaism: Practice & Belief 63 B.C.E.-66 C.E.*, by E. P. Sanders (Trinity Press International, 1998); page 278.
[2]From "The Book of Exodus," by Walter Brueggemann in *The New Interpreter's Bible* (Abingdon Press, 1994).
[3]In the Synoptic Gospels, the Temple scene comes much later in the narrative (Matthew 21:12-13; Mark 11:15-19; Luke 19:45-48).

Seeing God at Work

Scriptures for Lent:
The Fourth Sunday
Numbers 21:4-9
Ephesians 2:1-10
John 3:14-21

In the seven-hour drive to visit family, my sons and I often encounter road construction. Long before seeing road crews, we see the warning signs. I have often thought that it would be helpful if God would do the same. Think how reassuring it would be if everywhere we looked we saw giant orange signs announcing, "God at work!"

As Christians, we know that God is at work in our world, our churches, and our lives. Christ is present whenever the hungry are fed, the thirsty are given water, the naked are clothed, the sick are cared for, the imprisoned are visited (Matthew 23:35-45). Where, though, in the travesty of war is the God of peace? Where amid the millions of hungry is the God of fishes and loaves? Where in the tsunami is the God who stills the waters?

In the church, we may ask, where in times of division is the God of harmony? Where in the times of budgetary drought is the God who changes water to wine? Where for a dying church is the God of resurrection?

In our individual lives, we may become too busy or distracted to notice God's presence. We may be facing a decision and truly not know the more faithful path. Following consistently and faithfully would be so much easier if we were given signs—preferably large, orange, glow-in-the-dark signs.

Our three Lenten passages help us to recognize what in the world God is doing. Sometimes God works in spectacular ways, as evidenced in Numbers 21:4-9. Sometimes God works through ordinary signs of grace, as attested in Ephesians 2:1-10. John 3:14-21 helps to give us eyes to see signs of eternal life. As we examine these texts, we will also discuss spiritual disciplines that can help us to focus on what in the world, what in the church, and what in our hearts God is doing.

SPECTACULAR SIGNS
Numbers 21:4-9

As my sons and I were returning to Kansas City from a Christmas visit to my parents in central Illinois, we encountered construction-related delays. As we crawled down the interstate, I saw an exit sign for Highway 9, which is an alternate route to I-55, the next leg of our journey. Two signs indicated our options: 9 West or 9 East. With no map in the car, I chose 9 West since Kansas is west of Illinois.

The people in the Book of Numbers were on their own wilderness journey. In fact, the Hebrew name of the book is not *Numbers* but *Bemidbar*, which means "in the wilderness." Numbers is the story of the people of Israel as they traveled in the wilderness toward the freedom of Canaan.

Wilderness is a strong metaphor throughout Scripture. Wilderness denotes a place of transition (Exodus 13:20-23), of promise (Isaiah 43:19), of preparation (Matthew 3:1; Mark 1:3; Luke 3:2-4; John 1:23), of testing (Matthew 4:1; Mark 1:12; Luke 4:1), a place outside the center of power (Luke 7:24). The wilderness is an apt metaphor for our Lenten journeys as we allow God to lead us, through preparation and testing, to become the people God is calling us to be.

The wilderness was a fitting metaphor for the authors of Numbers. The book in its present form is believed to have been shaped after Babylonian exile (587-39 B.C.), itself a form of wilderness. The post-exilic era was a time of transition for Israel as those in exile and their descendants reunited with those who had been allowed to stay in Judah. Yahweh's people, separated by geography, cultural experiences, and generational differences, had the challenge of finding ways to live faithfully together without the Temple, which had been their unifying place of divine encounter, atonement, and revelation.

Imagine the division among the people: Exiles wanting to sing the contemporary worship songs they had sung in Babylon, Judah wanting to stay with the hymnal; exiles wanting to wear casual wilderness wear, Judah wanting to dress up as usual; exiles wanting the fancy drinks they had come to appreciate, Judah happy with the silver urn.

How does Numbers portray the people of God on their wilderness journey to the place of promise? God's people started out obedient and faithful (Numbers 1–10) but turned disobedient and rebellious (Chapters 11–20). Their journey became long, tedious, and difficult.

As our text begins, roadblocks (20:20-21) had caused a frustrating detour. The travelers became "impatient" (21:4). They complained "against God and against Moses" about inadequate food and water (Exodus 16:7). This is a particularly serious complaint. Previously they had complained about Moses but not directly to God (Numbers 14:27, 36). I can imagine Moses rolling his eyes as the kids in back whined, "Are we there yet?" and complained about the boring travel snacks.

No sooner did Israel leave Sinai than the people became consistently disobedient to God (11:1, 4-6; 14:2-4; 16:13-14; 20:3-5). God responded to their disobedience with judgment, sending "poisonous" or fiery snakes that bit the Israelites, causing some to die (21:6). As they had earlier (14:40), Israel responded to God's judgment by confessing their sin and asking Moses to pray for deliverance, which Moses did (verse 7).

Like any parent on a long trip with disgruntled passengers, Moses must have been at the end of his rope. He had already given his "how many times do I have to tell you?" lecture (14:41-43), and still they had not listened (14:44). Consequently, Israel had to suffer the consequences of their rebellion in military defeat (14:45).

Still, God answered Moses' prayer (21:7-8). God instructed Moses to "make a poisonous serpent and set it on a pole; and everyone who is bitten shall look at it and live" (verse 8). Moses did so. He "made a serpent of bronze and put it upon a pole" (verse 9). Whenever anyone was bitten by a snake, they could "look at the serpent of bronze and live" (verse 9). Israel was given an option: The snake could remain a means of death, or it could become a sign of healing.

We worship a God who gives us choice, as stated in Deuteronomy 30:19. "I have set before you life and death, blessings and curses. Choose life so that you and your descendants may live." Choice is not something we exercise only at the moment of conversion. We make choices all along our faith journey. We can choose to set our sights on that which heals or that which destroys. We can choose between obedience and disobedience.

Often, we choose poorly. Like the Israelites, we encounter roadblocks of distraction, division, doubt, and despair. We detour off the faithful path.

The good news is that we can participate with God who desires to transform our hearts and minds into the people God would have us be. We can participate by choosing to practice spiritual disciplines. In his book *Celebration of Discipline*, Richard Foster explains that spiritual disciplines are "the means by which we place ourselves where [God] can bless us."[1] By engaging in spiritual disciplines, such as prayer, study, meditation, fasting, simplicity, service, confession, and worship, we allow God to shape us into people who choose more faithful ways of living.

As part of an athlete's training, he or she will repeatedly go through drills so that in the game, the muscles will respond as they have been conditioned to do. By putting ourselves in a place to be blessed and transformed through the practice of spiritual disciplines, we willingly take a detour from the busy-ness of life for some wilderness time with God. In intentional time set apart to study Scripture, meditate, and pray, we give God time and space to transform us by the "renewing of our minds" (Romans 12:2).

The people in Numbers engaged in the discipline of confession, confessing their sin to Moses. Confession can be corporate as a part of worship or individual as a result of prayerful self-examination. Foster states, "In acts of mutual confession we release the power that heals. Our humanity is no longer denied, but transformed."[2] In Numbers, the people's confession led to Moses' prayer for God's transformation of the situation.

Prayer is another key spiritual discipline. Henri Nouwen says that prayer is "standing in the presence of God with the mind in the heart; that is at that point of our being where there are no divisions or distinctions and where we are totally one. . . . There heart speaks to heart, because there we stand before the face of the Lord, all-seeing within us."[3] Confession and Moses' prayer led to God's spectacular sign of healing.

As for my sons and me, we had traveled two and a half hours west on Highway 9 but had not run into I-55. When I finally stopped at a remote gas station for reassurance, I was told that, sure enough, Highway 9 runs right into I-55: "Just go about 3 hours east (from where we had just come!); you'll run right into it." Clearly, seeing the signs is not enough; there is also the crucial matter of going in the right direction!

How would you describe your faith journey? What have been key landmarks along the way?

What are the roadblocks that inhibit your spiritual growth?

How do the disciplines of confession and prayer contribute to your spiritual healing?

ORDINARY SIGNS OF GRACE
Ephesians 2:1-10

I did not look forward to telling my road-weary sons that we would be driving a total of five hours just to get back to our starting point. I anticipated anger. What I did not expect was eleven-year-old Timmy's response, "Yea! We get to go back to Grandma's!" His idea made sense. My parents welcomed us back with surprise and delight, and we made the most of an additional night's stay. Grace abounded.

Our epistle text begins with Paul reminding Christians how they had once been going in the wrong direction before God made them alive in Christ[4]: "You were dead through the trespasses and sins in which you once lived, following . . . the ruler of the power of the air, the spirit that is now at work among those who are disobedient" (Ephesians 2:1-2).

Power was a key issue for Paul. He believed that there were two ages: the Now and the Not Yet. The Not Yet is the "age to come" when God will complete God's purposes by establishing God's reign over creation. With Christ's resurrection, the Not Yet has broken into the present. Believers in Christ live in the in-between time, the time in the overlap of the ages. In this in-between time, humans choose with which power they will be aligned. Here, Paul says that previously, followers were serving the wrong power—one that was not life-giving.

Powers still compete for allegiance in the present. We have many choices for ways that we spend our money and time. Paul reminds against aligning with powers that are contrary to God's purposes. We, or others, may have succumbed to life-denying powers, such as addictions, unhealthy relationships, or the effects of greed. We, or others, may be going through the motions of life, missing the blessing of participating in God's power and purposes.

Paul elaborates the effects of these powers: "All of us once lived among them in the passions of our flesh, following the desires of flesh and senses, and we were by nature children of wrath, like everyone else" (verse 3). For Paul,

"flesh" did not allude only to sexual sins. Flesh represented all that was opposed to God. Important is Paul's understanding of the universality of sin. We all sin. "There is no one righteous, not even one" (Romans 3:10).

The good news? We, who were once under the power of sin, are now under the power of grace. In God's goodness, God has healed/saved us by the power of the Resurrection and placed us on the road of redemption (Ephesians 2:4-7). The destination is life with God in the Not Yet "so that in the ages to come God might show the immeasurable riches of his grace in kindness toward us in Christ Jesus" (verse 7). For Paul, Christ's resurrection is the guarantee that God will bring God's purposes to fruition. Christ's life, death, and resurrection—Christ's journey of faith—provides the promise for our journeys today.

In addition to providing the promise of destination, God has initiated and empowered our journey of healing and salvation: "For by grace you have been saved through faith, and this is not your own doing; it is the gift of God—not the result of works, so that no one may boast" (verses 8-9). It is belief in, and commitment to, God's purposes that enables us to be on this journey of faith.

The passage concludes by reminding God's people whose they are and what they are called to do: We are "created in Christ

Jesus for good works, which God prepared beforehand to be our way of life: (verses 10). God has graciously called God's people to the road of faithful obedience and service, a road that leads to life.

Disciplines of confession and listening prayer can open our hearts and minds to opportunities to participate in the discipline of service. True service is performed with the recipient's best interests in the fore, not our needs to build self-worth. For that reason, honest, prayerful discernment about our motives as well as God's purposes is necessary. Often the discipline of service is best performed *with* others instead of *for* others so that no one is placed in a subservient position. God-led rather than ego-led service should benefit all. Foster says, "True service builds community. It quietly and unpretentiously goes about caring for the needs of others. It draws, binds, heals, builds."[5]

As we participate in God's purposes for the good of creation, our eyes are opened to everyday acts of grace that surround us. It is as if God has already planned the generalities of our journey: We are "created in Christ Jesus for good works which God prepared beforehand to be our way of life" (verse 10). Through prayer, confession, and service, we work with God to navigate the particularities of our individual journeys.

What will the everyday, ordinary signs of grace along the way look like? Isaiah gives us a postcard view: "Thus says the LORD: In a time of favor I have answered you, on a day of salvation I have helped you; I have kept you and given you as a covenant to the people, to establish the land, to apportion the desolate heritages; saying to the prisoners, 'Come out,' to those who are in darkness, 'Show yourselves.' They shall feed along the ways, on all the bare heights shall be their pasture; they shall not hunger or thirst, neither scorching wind nor sun shall strike them down, for he who has pity on them will lead them, and by springs of water will guide them. And I will turn all my mountains into a road, and my highways shall be raised up" (Isaiah 49:8-11).

What powers can you identify that are not life-giving?

How does God's power and presence free us from imprisoning powers? What people or organizations provide assistance to those wanting to be freed from oppressive situations?

Think of examples of true service you have engaged in. What were some signs of grace you experienced along the way?

SIGNS OF (ETERNAL) LIFE
John 3:14-21

It was not for a lack of signs that my sons and I headed in the wrong direction for two and a half hours. We saw plenty of 9 West signs along the way. The problem was our interpretation of these signs. Anyone with a more informed understanding of that part of the state would have seen the signs and realized they needed to turn around. Just seeing signs is not enough.

The community that John's Gospel originally addressed needed signs of God's activity in their world, their church, and their lives. Recall that John's Gospel was written around A.D. 80, about a decade after Roman forces had sacked Jerusalem and destroyed the Temple. John's struggling community of mostly Jewish-Christians were trying to find their way of being faithful at a time when many faithful Jews were debating about what faithfulness now looked like.

The Temple had been the place where God's presence was encountered, atonement received, and God's will made known. How faithfulness was now to be lived out was a subject of controversy, causing division in the synagogue (John 9:22; 12:42; 16:2). Under the power of Roman rule in post-Temple times, John's community could have interpreted the signs to mean God is off duty, or worse, God has been defeated by the Roman gods. However, these people of faith interpreted the signs a different way.

In John's Gospel, there are numerous signs of God's power and presence. *Sign* is the term John used for a miracle. The Gospel writer asserted that miracles are not, in themselves, the object of focus. The signs need to be understood as wondrous deeds that point to the power and presence of God. In John, they are signs of God's glory. By the third chapter, Jesus' signs have gotten people's attention. The first sign was changing water to wine at the wedding in Cana (2:11). The Jews asked Jesus for a sign regarding the Temple incident discussed in the previous chapter (2:18). Many believed in Jesus because of the signs he was doing (2:23). Jesus' signs got the attention of Nicodemus, who came to Jesus by night. Jesus was responding to Nicodemus's statement about Jesus' signs in 3:14-21.

Jesus explained to Nicodemus the importance of perspective and understanding in interpreting his signs: "No one can see the kingdom of God without being born from above" (verse 3). Nicodemus was clearly going in the wrong direction with his thoughts: "How can anyone be born after having grown old? Can one enter a second time into the mother's womb and be born?" (verse 4). Jesus explained that one's perspective is everything: "You must be born from above" (verse 7). Where one stands determines what one sees. Jesus tried to illuminate Nicodemus's perspective of faith. Jesus wanted him to understand the ultimate sign—Jesus' crucifixion, resurrection, and ascension that was to come.

Jesus has just explained that his origin makes him unique: "No one has ascended into heaven except the one who descended from heaven, the Son of Man" (verse 13). It matters from where one has come. Jesus has come from God and will return to God.

Jesus said, "Just as Moses lifted up the serpent in the wilderness, so must the Son of Man be lifted up." This is the first of three times in the Gospel that Jesus used the phrase "lifting up" to reveal his crucifixion/resurrection/ascension (also 8:28; 12:32-34). In John, the three events are understood as one event that "glorifies" Jesus (7:39). Jesus wanted to put the event in the context of other spectacular signs God had performed for God's people. He compared Moses' lifting up of the serpent to God's lifting up of Jesus. Just as God was present with God's people on their wilderness journey to the Promised Land of Canaan, God was with God's people in John's community. Just as God's people could look at Moses' serpent and be healed, so those in John's community could choose to see the healing power of the glorified Jesus.

Jesus continued by explaining the consequence of his being lifted up—"that whoever believes in him may have eternal life" (3:15). There are many ideas about what eternal life will be like. John has his own definition: Eternal life is life lived in communion with God and Jesus (17:3). Eternal life is knowing God, encountering God, and experiencing God.

We can more clearly know God if we more fully understand God's purposes, which Jesus elaborated in John 3:16: "For God so loved the world that he gave his only Son, so that everyone who believes in him may not perish but may have eternal life." In John, eternal life is not something that is Not Yet. Eternal life is *Now*. It is a matter of choice, a matter of perspective. Perspective is determined by whether we choose to recognize the holy presence of God and Jesus through the Spirit. All are offered this invitation, for God intends to save the entire world (verse 17).

This passage acknowledges that some are condemned, even though that is not God's intention (verse 17). Whether one is condemned depends on one's belief: "Those who believe in him are not condemned; but those who do not believe are condemned already" (verse 18). It is essential to understand what John meant by "belief."

John used the verb "to believe" 98 times. (If it is repeated, sit up and take notice!) In Greek, the word for "belief" also means "faith." Though the word is often used as a noun, John used it only as a verb. For John, faithful belief was an active, dynamic process. Faith is not something someone *has*; it is what someone *does*. Believing is not a decision that is made once upon a time. Believing is a continuous decision, an action one continually makes along the journey of faith. As we participate with God in God's good purposes, we experience God, Jesus, and the Spirit. It is in acts of believing that we know, see, touch, taste, and experience signs of life.

Judgment, then, is a personal choice, made because "people loved darkness rather than light because their deeds were evil" (verse 19). In the Prologue, the Gospel tells of people that chose to turn away from the light (1:10-11). Jesus acknowledged that there are powers contrary to God's purposes in the world (12:31; 14:30; 16:11; 17:15).

The passage concludes by reassuring all who are surrounded by dark powers contrary to God's purposes: "But those who do what is true come to the light, so that it may be clearly seen that their deeds have been done in God" (3:21). It is through faithful, believing actions that we allow ourselves to be placed in God's light, one decision at a time.

John's Gospel offers John's community a perspective by which to explain the circumstances of division, dissension, and devastation in their midst. Even though all evidence may seem to the contrary, God is sovereign. God is faithful to God's life-giving, liberating, loving purposes. You can see for yourself, if you know how to interpret the signs. Even better, you can participate in God's purposes. Jesus is the new temple (2:19-22). By living in communion with Jesus and God through the power of the Spirit, you will become the locus of God's activity (14:15-31).

How can we stay in the light and avoid being overtaken by the darkness of doubt, despair, division, and distraction? Again, spiritual disciplines can help us to keep our focus.

In addition to the disciplines of confession, prayer, and service, another crucial discipline is study. Foster states, "The purpose of the Spiritual Disciplines is the total transformation of the person. They aim at replacing old destructive habits of thought with new life-giving habits. Nowhere is this purpose more clearly seen than in the Discipline of study."[6] Thoughtful, consistent reading of Scripture reshapes us into the image of the Word. As Marjorie Thompson says, "When we are engaged in spiritual reading it is not so much we who read the Word as the Word who 'reads' us!"[7]

Through disciplines such as study, prayer, confession, and service, we learn to recognize God's nature and purposes and how they are manifest in our lives, our churches, and our world. Sometimes the signs are spectacular. Segregation ends. Apartheid is no more. The Berlin Wall comes down. Sometimes the signs are ordinary. A boy hugs his grandma. A worst-case scenario works out for the best. The darkness gives way to light. All are signs along the journey of faith.

As my sons and I can attest, the journey is more enjoyable when going in the right direction. Knowing the destination helps. Best of all is the power and presence of the One who accompanies us always, the One who equips and empowers us as we tread the path before us.

Maybe we do not always need to *see* signs of God's work. Maybe we are called to *be* signs of God's activity.

As we continue our Lenten journey, may our lives be shaped so that we manifest the meaning of Jesus' life, death, and resurrection in our hearts, our churches, and our world.

Think of decisions you have made. What are signs that you were (or were not) heading in a faithful direction?

In what spiritual disciplines is God calling you to participate?

How do you experience eternal life in communion with God, Jesus, and the Holy Spirit?

[1] From *Celebration of Discipline: The Path to Spiritual Growth*, by Richard Foster (Harper and Row, 1988); page 7.

[2] From *Celebration of Discipline*, page 146.

[3] From *The Way of the Heart*, by Henri J. M. Nouwen (Ballantine Books, 1991); pages 59-60.

[4] Scholars disagree over issues such as authorship (whether Paul or a follower composed the letter), audience, and date of composition. The message, though, is characteristically Pauline. I will refer to the author as *Paul*.

[5] From *Celebration of Discipline*, pages 129-30.

[6] From *Celebration of Discipline*, page 62.

[7] From *Soul Feast: An Invitation to the Christian Spiritual Life*, by Marjorie J. Thompson (Westminster John Knox Press, 1995); page 20.

Seeing Ways to Thrive

Scriptures for Lent: The Fifth Sunday
Jeremiah 31:31-34
Hebrews 5:5-10
John 12:20-33

I remember the April afternoon I visited Gretchen's home. She had invited me to visit on the last weekend before her move to an assisted-living facility. Coming in her front door, I was embraced by the warm hospitality I had also experienced regularly in my grandma's house. Gretchen's smile lit up her comfortable living room. I followed in interest as she showed me around. We lingered in every room as she shared memories of her last 54 years. The kitchen, tidy in its simplicity, had been the place where hundreds of Easter dinners, Christmas goodies, birthday cakes, and evening suppers had been prepared. The dining room table, with its hand-crocheted tablecloth, had been the gathering place for countless breakfasts, dinners, and celebrations. On the bedside table beside her quilt-covered bed was a handsome picture of Gretchen and her husband—"for the church directory," she said. Walt, her husband of 46 years, had died eight years earlier.

As we sat down to drink iced tea, Gretchen talked of Walt, the home and life they had created, and the four children they had raised. She and her family had decided that she would move to a place that offered more assistance and care. Still, the decision grieved her deeply.

"I cannot imagine how it must be to leave your home of more than 50 years," I said. She nodded as tears clouded her eyes. Then she said, "But I'm not leaving it. I'm taking it with me"; and her hands closed over her heart.

Sometimes circumstances present themselves that we would not necessarily choose. Sometimes we wish our choices were different. Our texts help us to see ways to thrive, even in circumstances beyond our choosing, by viewing life through the perspective of faith. Jeremiah 31:31-34 helps us to see from the perspective of the heart. Hebrews 5:5-10 sets our sights on the life, death, and resurrection of Christ. John 12:20-33 offers a perspective on longing for the home we find in God. Taken together, these texts help us to watch and pray for ways that we can thrive, empowered by God's power as we participate in God's purposes.

SEEING THROUGH THE HEART
Jeremiah 31:31-34

Throughout this study, we have witnessed the ongoing trauma of exile (587-39 B.C.). Now we see an up close and personal glimpse of Babylonian capture and the series of deportations offered to us by the prophet Jeremiah. From 597 B.C. when Judah revolted against Babylon to the Babylonian invasions and deportations of 587 and 582 B.C., Jeremiah provided the perspective of an "embedded reporter." Unlike a reporter, though, Jeremiah did not do objective, detached reporting. Instead, he bore the pain of his people, making him a profound symbol of Judah's devastation and restoration.

When Jeremiah received his call and commission from God, he first protested before accepting it (1:4-19). What was Jeremiah called to do? He was to "pluck up and to pull down, / to destroy and to overthrow, / to build and to plant" (1:10).

We work so hard to build and to create. We put our hearts and souls into making a home for our loved ones, building a career to finance our dreams. Our churches create ministries intended to better the lives of God's people. It is easy to feel God's presence when things are going well and we see evidence of growth. When the fruits of our labors are "plucked up and pulled down," however, when that which we have created is "destroyed and overthrown," it can be harder to believe that we are on a faithful path. Jeremiah offered this glimpse of another way in which God is working for the good of all creation.

Jeremiah chose to look at the events that transpired—Babylonians crashing through the city walls, burning the Temple, killing scores of people—not through the lens of fear but through the lens of faith. He chose to frame all that happened in the context of God's power and purposes. He interpreted the destruction and deportation as evidence of God's judgment against people who had failed to live their part of the covenantal agreement, which he compared to a marriage covenant (Chapter 2). Rather than giving testimony to the weakness of God against the powers of Babylon, Jeremiah asserted that exile was part of God's plan for a people who had not been faithful to God's purposes (Chapters 1–25).

Jeremiah had long focused on the sins of the people. In his own

"Temple incident," he railed against injustices being perpetuated by the nation (7:1-15) and the people (7:16-8:3). He offered numerous confessions on behalf of the people (11:18-12:4; 15:10-21; 17:14-18; 18:18-23; 20:7-13-18), but Jeremiah's focus did not remain on judgment.

Along with being the voice of judgment, Jeremiah offered the voice of hope (26:1–52:34). The God who plucks up and pulls down also builds and plants. Jeremiah asserted that the nations, though judged, could survive; in fact, they could thrive. The thriving of God's people has to do with God's identity and purposes. God intends for the redemption of God's people so that they may participate in God's purposes for the flourishing of all creation.

It is time to look forward, Jeremiah said. After focusing on the sin of the past and the devastation of the present exile (10:17-25; 15:1-9; 25:1-38), Jeremiah encouraged the people to look ahead toward the future, a future based on the promises of God (23:1-8; 26:1–52:34, especially Chapters 30–31).

When days are at their darkest, it can be difficult to imagine brighter times. Immersed in the darkness of winter, it is hard to believe that the sunshine of spring will once again coax daffodils from their depths. Jeremiah addressed people in the midst of their pain, in the valley of their shadows, and told them of the glorious future they had in God. The essence of hope would come in the form of a new covenant.

"The days are surely coming, says the LORD, when I will make a new covenant with the house of Israel and the house of Judah" (31:31). The focus had shifted. God's attention was not on the people's sin and the subsequent punishment of exile. God's attention was on a new way that God would relate to the people God had redeemed.

Spiritual disciplines enable us to place ourselves in a position for God to illuminate our focus on the sin inherent to the human condition. The Lenten season is a good time to enter into the discipline of prayerful meditation, asking God to reveal areas and consequences of our brokenness. We confess:

> Most merciful God, we confess that we have sinned against you in thought, word, and deed, by what we have done, and by what we have left undone. We have not loved you with our whole heart; we have not loved our neighbors as ourselves. We are truly sorry and we humbly repent. For the sake of your Son Jesus Christ, have mercy on us and forgive us; that we may delight in your will, and walk in your ways, to the glory of your name. Amen.[1]

Thankfully, we do not have to remain in our sin. We confess to a God who has forgiven our sin and seeks to restore us to right relationship with God and with one another. God redeems God's people, as Jeremiah proclaimed. In this text, God's redemption is expressed in a "new covenant" with God's people (verse 31). God's new covenant did not abolish the old covenant with Israel, nor was it referring to the covenant God would make with Christians through Christ. Christians, in reading the Old Testament through Jesus-lenses, rightly see faith in Jesus as continuous with God's covenant with Israel. In this Old Testament passage, however, Jeremiah was speaking specifically of God's renewed and restored relationship between God and Israel.

In explaining this new covenant, Jeremiah evoked the covenant made at Sinai (Exodus 19–Numbers 11). The people had refused to honor their covenantal commitments "though I was their husband, says the LORD" (Jeremiah 31:32; see also 2:2). It was not God who had broken covenant; God had remained faithful to Israel.

The passage continued by explaining the different way God and God's people would now relate: "I will put my law within them, and I will write it on their hearts" (31:33). The law would become part of them—forming, shaping their identity as a people.

As my sons were growing up, we had some bad days when the boys would argue relentlessly and my patience was shot. In such times, any one of us could say, "Do-overs." That was our signal that we recognized what we had been doing and acknowledged our need to wipe the slate clean and begin again. Sometimes I would even say, "Good morning" late in the afternoon—signaling that as of that moment, it was a new day.

The new covenant is God's fresh start for God's people: Same family, same God, same covenantal commitments—but an opportunity to begin again with a clean slate.

A fresh start, a clean slate, is available to us every moment through God's grace. Through spiritual disciplines such as prayer, confession, study, service, meditation, fasting, and worship, we can become more aware of God's promises and purposes that are to be written on our hearts.

God promised to write on Israelite hearts, "I will be their God and they shall be my people" (verse 33). God wanted Israel (and us) to know—down to the core of our being—who God is and who we are. God is the sovereign, faithful covenant-maker who can realign our purposes so that we desire and work toward the flourishing of creation. We are God's people, called to participate in God's purposes. This is the lens through which we, as Christians, should view every circumstance, every decision, every feeling, every disappointment, and every person. This promise extends to everyone—for all will "know [God], from the least of them to the greatest" (verse 34).

All can know God in a new way. All can know God as one in whom grace, not judgment, is ultimate. God now sees the Jews not through the lens of disobedience but through the lens of God's covenant of grace. The Lord said, "I will forgive their iniquity, and remember their sin no more" (verse 34). No longer are those who have sinned a prisoner of their past. Because of God's forgiving nature, because of God's purposes for the flourishing of all creation, God extends the invitation of present and future glory to all.

Seeing ourselves through God's eyes is not easy for those of us who more readily see ourselves through the lens of shame or harsh societal standards. Verse 33 promises that we will be given God's law. God "will write it on [our] hearts." Through prayer, meditation, and quiet times with God, we can live into the truth God has placed in us. We can more deeply understand that before we were born, God "beheld [our] unformed substance. In [God's] book were written all the days that were formed for [us], when none of them as yet existed" (Psalm 139:16).

Where one stands often determines what one sees. When standing on the promises of God, we can look to God's future hope that overcomes our past sin and present despair. It comes down to a perspective of faith—seeing our circumstances through more than just our eyes. As Augustine said, "Our whole business in this life is to heal this eye of the heart whereby God may be seen."[2]

My brave friend Gretchen saw God accompanying her on every step of her new journey, her prayers being answered in small and spectacular ways. In the grief of leaving her beloved home, she could see glimpses of future hope, telling me about the flowering crabapple tree that would blossom right outside her new living room window. She planned to hang a birdfeeder on its branches. She was taking to this new place the feeling of home and the hope of God she carried in her heart.

How have you been formed and shaped in God's law? What is written on your heart?

Imagine God saying to your church, "I will be your God, and you will be my people." What does this mean for you?

Today, who would be "the least" and "the greatest" who will know God?

What does it mean to follow and serve a God who forgives iniquities and remembers sins no more? Wherein lies the grace and challenge of this promise for your life?

SETTING OUR SIGHTS ON CHRIST
Hebrews 5:5-10

Life can lead to journeys we would not necessarily choose. Our second text evokes Jesus' journey to the cross. It frames Jesus' journey from life to death from the perspective of resurrection faith.

Much is unknown about the Letter to the Hebrews, including whether it is even a letter. It reads like a sermon (13:22), though its originator and audience are unknown. Also unclear is the date of composition, although many scholars agree that it was composed between A.D. 60 and 100. It seems the audience is struggling to remain faithful (10:25) through difficult circumstances (12:12). In exhorting faithfulness and perseverance on this difficult journey of faith, the text sets our sights on Christ.

As I waited in the doctor's office for a routine appointment yesterday, the nurse and I engaged in conversation. She and her husband are planning to move out of their home of 28 years. She loves her sprawling two-story home in which she and her husband raised their two sons, now 27 and 31. She can still remember the boys as toddlers, poised by their dad at the bathroom sink, watching in rapt attention as he shaved. They need to move, she said, because her husband's diabetes no longer allows him to climb stairs. "I feel so blessed to be a nurse," she said. "It is as if I have been appointed to be the one who has the privilege to care for him," she said. "At the same time, I worry if I have what it takes to get us through this."

I have heard it said that when you feel drawn towards a challenge yet want to run away, you can be sure you are in the presence of the holy. Certainly Jeremiah was reluctant in his call ("Truly I do not know how to speak, for I am only a boy," Jeremiah 1:6). Jeremiah was obedient; and God empowered Jeremiah to do God's work (Jeremiah 1:7-19), saying, "I am with you . . . to deliver you" (Jeremiah 1:19).

Jesus, too, was obedient even unto death. Jesus was chosen, commissioned, and anointed by God (Psalm 2:7; Hebrews 5:5). God's call to Jesus is consistent with God's call to other priests, such as Melchizedek (Psalm 110:4; Hebrews 5:6), who also have participated in God's purposes for the good of all creation.

By evoking Psalm 110 in which the name of the priest Melchizedek appears, the writer evoked not only the tradition of priesthood but also the assured victory of God through God's appointed agents. Psalm 110 is a royal psalm (as is Psalm 2) that assures readers of the victory of God's priest-king, a tradition to which Jesus as High Priest belongs. The faithful can indeed trust that "the LORD is at your right hand; he will shatter kings on the day of his wrath. He will execute judgment among the nations" (Psalm 110:5-6a).

The Lord was at Jesus' right hand as Jesus, in his obedience, called out in his suffering (Hebrews 5:7). As we know, suffering was not the end of the story. God made Jesus "perfect" or "complete" (The Greek word can be translated either way.), thereby becoming "the source of eternal salvation for all who obey him" (2:10; 5:9). Jesus lived out his calling as one appointed, anointed, "Christed" by God, consistent with Melchizedek (5:10). Melchizedek will be evoked yet again in Hebrews in reference to another model of obedient faithfulness, Abraham (Chapter 7).

For those who are struggling to fulfill difficult callings on the hard road of faith, Hebrews lifts up Jesus, appointed by God to fulfill God's purposes for the flourishing of all creation.

It is one thing to trust that Jesus fulfilled God's call, but we may be apprehensive about our calls. Each of us is called to fulfill tasks God has designated to us. When facing a daunting task or a move I did not choose, I often respond with hesitance ("I'm not sure I can do this.") or indignant protest ("God, what are you thinking?").

Our Hebrews text reminds us that when God calls us to new tasks, we can respond in humble obedience. We can trust that the One who raised Jesus from the dead will equip us as we face challenges and participate in God's purposes.

Can you recall a time when you felt drawn toward a challenge yet wanted to run the other way?

How has God empowered your church to do a task that seemed daunting? In what ways have you been equipped to participate in God's purposes?

How does knowing that victory has already been won (Psalm 110) affect your perspective?

LONGING FOR HOME
John 12:20-33

What makes a home? The question becomes important when, like Gretchen or the nurse and her husband, we must change residences. Recently, Timmy, my 11-year-old, asked me what I would take from our home if we had a fire. Without thinking, I said I would grab him and his brother. "But what else?" he asked. My list used to be longer. With moves and life changes, I have come to see that my list of essentials—what truly gives me life—is not that long. It is a list of people, not things. My concept of home relates to my sense of purpose. I believe a home should provide the surroundings for all who live there to do what they are called to do. Home is where everyone feels welcome and wanted.

John's Gospel addresses the concept of home. The Prologue reveals that Jesus never truly felt at home in this world because the world rejected him (1:10-11). In John, Jesus is presented in the Wisdom tradition. In another first-century Jewish writing, Wisdom is depicted as coming to earth and finding no resting place and returning to heaven (1 Enoch 42).

The idea of home was important to the community John's Gospel addressed around A.D. 80. The Temple, destroyed by Rome about ten years previously, had been a spiritual home in which God's presence was experienced, God's will was made known, and God's forgiveness was received. The loss of the Temple left Jews, as well as some Jewish followers of Christ feeling like exiles. The Temple destruction threatened to destroy the practices and traditions that were part of the Jewish heritage—practices that many persons in John's community had continued as they followed Jesus.

One way that post-70 Jewish Christians observed faithfulness was to worship in their homes. The last place Jesus visited before entering the festival in Jerusalem, where our text takes place, was a home. It was the home of Lazarus, whom Jesus raised from the dead (12:1). It was there that Mary anointed Jesus' feet in preparation for his burial (verses 3-8). Ironically, Jesus' gift of life to Lazarus incited the ruling elite to want to put Lazarus to death, too (verse 10).

It was into this escalating hostility that Jesus entered as he entered Jerusalem. Our passage begins with the appearance of "some Greeks" who wished to see Jesus (verses 21-21). In John, the verb "to see" often has to do with accepting or refusing to accept Jesus as the revealer of God (1:18,

33-34, 39; 3:3, 11, 32, 36; 5:37; 11:32, 40).

After this incident, Jesus announced the arrival of "the hour" (12:23). Throughout the Gospel, Jesus had spoken of an hour that now had come (2:4; 4:21, 23; 7:30; 8:20). Only now did Jesus make it clear that the hour had to do with "the Son of Man [being] glorified" (12:23).

When John spoke of Jesus as the "Son of Man," he implied several things.[3] The Son of Man was the man from Nazareth who performed signs of God's glory (9:35-38). The Son of Man was residing in this world temporarily: His home was in heaven, he descended to participate in God's purposes, and he would again ascend to heaven after he had completed his task (3:13; 6:62; 16:28). The Son of Man had been sent by God the Father (3:34; 4:34; 8:25; 9:4). Also the Son of Man would be "glorified," as 12:23 attests.

In John, to participate in God's glory is to experience God's power and presence (1:14; 2:11; 11:4). Jesus had foretold his glorification (7:39). Now he was saying that the time for his glorification had come. Jesus was shining light on his crucifixion, which, in John, was not an isolated event. The Crucifixion was one part of the "lifting up" that included Crucifixion/Resurrection/Ascension (3:14; 8:28; 12:32). Jesus' crucifixion did not mean that Rome had out-powered God. The Crucifixion cannot be isolated from the Resurrection and the Ascension. To try to discuss one without the other is to see only part of the story. In John, to see the crucifixion/resurrection/ascension of Jesus is to see the power and presence of God.

John's community, then, was offered a new perspective on their former religious home, the Temple. The decimated Temple was not evidence of Rome's power. It was evidence of God's action to "destroy and to overthrow" so that God was able "to build and to plant" (Jeremiah 1:10). The Jewish Temple had been replaced by the new temple of Jesus, the new home for believers (John 2:19-22). The passage illustrates God's power to redeem even death: If "a single grain . . . dies, it bears much fruit" (12:24). The notion that there can be redemption in death goes against our sensibilities. It is easier to see God's power and presence in the building up and the planting. When that which is before us is plucked up and pulled down, when it is destroyed and overthrown, it is harder to believe that "all things can work together for good for those who love God, who are called according to his purpose" (Romans 8:28). Yet, the good news is that there can be good even in death.

How can this be? How can a God who is life-giving and loving allow death? The passage goes on, "Those who love their life lose it, and those who hate their life in this world will keep it for eternal life" (John 12:25). For John, God loves the world (3:16), though the world sometimes represents those who refuse to believe in Jesus (7:7). The world is different from heaven, Jesus' place of origin (8:23). Additionally, life in this world is different from eternal life. In John, eternal life is life lived in communion with Jesus and God (17:3). The good news in John is that eternal life can be experienced any time, even in this world (5:24). What, then, does life lived in communion with Jesus and God look like?

To live with God and Jesus is to live in service to God and one another (12:26). It is to follow faithfully even when the journey takes us where we would rather not go. Jesus illustrated this in his journey to the cross, a journey that "troubled" his soul (verse 27). It was a journey that Jesus obediently took, a journey in which God was "glorified" (verse 28). (Sit up and take notice; "glorify" is repeated three times in verse 28!) Jesus framed the crucifixion—the worst that Rome could do—in light of the resurrection and the ascension. The power of Rome was no match for the power of God.

It appears that Jesus had his own short list of what is essential—what he would take with him as he left the world (verse 33). On his list were people—all people: "I, when I am lifted up from the earth, will draw all people to myself" (verse 32). In the same way that

I would not leave my burning house without my kids, Jesus did not want to leave this world without gathering all people to himself.

Jesus knew what it was like to make his home in a place that did not accept him, to have to leave home. Before he left, though, he wanted to teach his followers what home really was. Home is with him and God. Not only are we welcome and wanted there, but we are expected: "In my Father's house there are many dwelling places. If it were not so, would I have told you that I go to prepare a place for you? And if I go and prepare a place for you, I will come again and will take you to myself, so that where I am, there you may be also" (14:2-3).

In the words of Augustine, "Everlasting God, in whom we live and move and have our being: You have made us for Yourself, and our hearts are restless until they rest in You."

Are there ways that you feel out of place in your surroundings? How do God's power and presence affect your perspective?

Think of a past or present challenge in your personal or church life. How did you take on (or how could you have taken on) the role of a servant?

What in your life is God tearing down? What is God building up?

What does it mean to know that Jesus wants to draw you—and all people—to himself?

---

[1] *The United Methodist Hymnal* (United Methodist Publishing House, 1989); 890.
[2] From "Sermon XXXVIII: On the Words of the Gospel, Matthew XX 30, About the Two Blind Men Sitting By the Way Side, and Crying Loud, 'Lord Have Mercy on Us, Thou Son of David,'" in *Sermons on Selected Lessons of the New Testament*, by Saint Augustine of Hippo.
[3] From *John: The Maverick Gospel*, by Robert Kysar (Westminster John Knox Press, 1993); pages 40-41.

Recognizing Threats

We are surrounded by threats and warnings. The Terror Alert System has become the refrain of our national existence. Other warnings exist as well. Tornado, hurricane, severe thunderstorm, flood, and, now, tsunami warnings alert us to danger. We are attuned to the signals. A Terror Alert of yellow means the threat is "Elevated"; Orange means "High." A tornado siren instructs to take cover. A tsunami warning directs to higher ground.

We know about medical warnings, too. Chest discomfort and shortness of breath can signal a heart attack. Sudden numbness or vision difficulty can indicate a stroke. A hand to the throat indicates choking. Extreme thirst may indicate diabetes. Inability to focus may be signaling A.D.D. We learn to recognize signals of distress and danger so that we can contribute to the survival and care of others as well as ourselves.

Threats and warnings pervaded the world in which the biblical texts were composed as well. Each of our three passages concerns threats. In Mark 11:1-11, Jesus' entry into Jerusalem continues to reveal the threat that Jesus' alternative way of being and doing was to the status quo of the Roman Empire. In Isaiah 50:4-9, the third servant song demonstrates a way to respond to threats to those who participate in God's purposes. In the Passion Narrative of Mark 15:1-47, we see how Rome dealt with the threat Jesus presented to the status quo of the Roman Empire.

By recognizing God's purposes, we can better recognize that which threatens God's purposes. By also recognizing the threat that God's purposes are to the status quo, we can understand the fear that fuels resistance to God's purposes.

Our continued Lenten prayer is that our eyes be opened to the ways in which we are called to participate in God's life-giving, loving, liberating purposes. Our prayer is that we, like Jesus, can make inroads of change as we journey toward the goal of the flourishing of all creation.

MAKING INROADS
Mark 11:1-11

When Mark's Gospel was written around A.D. 70, discipleship was a threatening way of life. Mark's audience was probably a hard-pressed community of Jewish Christians living in Rome while Rome and Judea were at war. The threat to Jewish followers of Jesus increased after A.D. 70 when Rome overtook Jerusalem and decimated the Temple. The significant place at which Jews encountered God, atoned for sins, and discerned God's will was no more.

All of this occurred only 40 years after Rome had crucified Jesus. Threats abounded. A few years earlier, in 64, Roman emperor Nero killed Christians in Rome. There had been a terrible fire, which, it is said, Nero himself started. To deflect blame, he ordered that Christians be put to death. This was, however, an isolated event, not an empire-wide practice. Still, the Nero incident was a reminder of Rome's power and ability to govern according to the whims of the elite. Mark alludes to Rome's power as well: "As for yourselves, beware; for they will hand you over to councils; and you will be beaten in synagogues;

and you will stand before governors and kings because of me, as a testimony to them" (13:9).

In addition to political issues, there was the ongoing threat to well-being that Roman rule presented. Goods and services, taxes and rents supplied by peasants and artisans sustained the lavish lifestyles of the ruling elite. Imposed taxation, up to 70 percent of a peasant or artisan's production, perpetuated a system of injustice from which it became impossible for the majority to emerge. Inadequate nutrition, unclean water, insufficient medical care, and the grueling demands of day-to-day survival contributed to mental and physical ailments that plagued the underclass. Clearly, living under Roman rule was hazardous to the majority's health and well-being.[1]

Mark's Gospel gives evidence to the effects of Roman rule: demonic possession (1:23), disease (1:30), and death (5:23). The Gospel, though, boldly asserts that Rome could not dictate the ultimate consequence of destruction on God's people.

Mark asserted that even in the heart of the Roman Empire, Jesus, the agent of God's empire, had authority over demonic possession (1:27; 6:7), disease (1:34, 42), and death (5:41-42).

The "good news" in Mark's Gospel (1:1) is that God's kingdom or empire (the word is the same in Greek) is at hand (1:15). In the first ten chapters of the

Gospel, Jesus' teaching and healing made inroads into the destructive effects of the Roman Empire. Jesus cleansed unclean spirits (1:25-26; 9:14-29), healed (1:29-34; 40-45; 3:10; 5:1-20; 6:55-56; 8:22-25), forgave sins (2:5), taught (4:1-34; 10:1-12; 17-31), fed (6:30-44; 8:1-10), and blessed those whom society marginalized (10:13-16). Jesus and his band of peasant followers (1:16-20) made threatening inroads into the Roman Empire's system of inequality and injustice.

In Mark 11, Jesus made his entry into Jerusalem. The way in which Jesus entered signaled differences between God's kingdom and Rome. Those with eyes to see recognized the threat that Jesus and his followers presented to systems that opposed God's purposes.

Jesus' entry into Jerusalem was not unlike Greco-Roman entrance processions. It was common in militaristic empires for a triumphal entry to consist of the appearance of the ruler with his troops. They would process into the city, greeted by celebrating crowds.

Jesus' entrance, however, contrasted with, even mocked that of Rome. Triumphal entries often signaled a political victory over enemies. Mark's account of the place of entry gives signals to an alert audience. Jesus came into the power center of Jerusalem "near the Mount of Olives" (11:1), the place of eschatological judgment and salvation (Zechariah 14:4). The act was a sign, as Zechariah foretold (Zechariah 14:1-20), that God's empire would ultimately triumph: "The LORD will become king over all the earth" (Zechariah 14:9).

The method of entry was another sign. Jesus rode in on a colt (Mark 11:2-7). The young donkey was one on which God's eschatological king rode in Zechariah 9:9: "Triumphant and victorious is he, humble and riding on a donkey, on a colt, the foal of a donkey." The colt differed from the chariot, which highlighted the emperor's prominence or war horse (Zechariah 9:10), which indicated military might. Jesus illustrated the difference between God's reign and Rome by parodying Rome's processions.

The crowd response gave another signal. As in Greco-Roman processions, the crowd welcomed and celebrated the person of honor. The crowd "threw their cloaks on [the colt]" Jesus sat on; others "spread their cloaks on the road," indicating Jesus' authority (11:7-8). To these people, Jesus—not the Roman emperor—was in charge. Their actions signaled their purpose as followers. They "spread leafy branches that they had cut in the fields" (verse 8). Branches were a sign of liberation when Judas Maccabeus rededicated the Temple after the tyranny of Antiochus Epiphanes ended (1 Maccabees 13:51).

The voice of the crowd gave further clues as to Jesus' purposes. Reciting Psalm 118:25-26, the crowd yelled, "Hosanna! Blessed is the one who comes in the name of the LORD!" (Mark 11:9). Psalm 118 is the conclusion of the Hallel psalms (113–118), which begin with the story of the Exodus and entry into the land and are sung at Passover. Psalm 118:15 gives thanks to God for victory in a "procession with branches" (Psalm 118:27). The crowd continued, "Blessed is the coming kingdom of our ancestor David!" (Mark 11:10). Jesus' coming kingdom is one in which God's purposes for the healing and flourishing of all will be victorious.

The crowd continued, "Hosanna [Save] in the highest heaven!" indicating that God is more powerful than Rome. God's coming empire has political, social, religious, and economic effects, as Jesus' entrance into the Temple indicated. In an incident reminiscent of Jeremiah 7, Jesus condemned the Temple for its unjust practices (Mark 11:15-18).

Jesus' alternative way of doing a triumphal procession underscored the alternative empire Jesus revealed. Jesus' acts of exorcizing, healing, teaching, feeding, and giving life had not gone unnoticed. The powers that be recognized the threat that God's power presented to their status quo. That is why the powerful elite worked to eliminate the threat Jesus presented (14:1).

In the time of Jesus, as when Mark's Gospel was written, Rome made the rules. The prevailing political power determined what kind of society would exist. Those, however, who aligned themselves to God's power found an alternative way to live within the empire. They participated in God's powers of liberation. They found a way to participate in life-giving practices. They found a way to overcome poverty, hunger, and disease. By participating in alternative ways of being and doing, a small, committed group of people threatened the Roman Empire.

We know what ultimately happened to Rome. The seemingly indomitable empire fell. God's empire continues in and through Jesus' followers. Jesus' entrance was just the beginning.

In what ways does our society highlight victories or successes?

How are God's purposes alike or counter to that of our society?

How are you as an individual or a part of a church community called to change practices that oppose God's purposes?

What does victory look like in the realm of faith? Can you think of small or major successes you have witnessed or in which you have participated?

CONFRONTING THREATS
Isaiah 50:4-9

We live in a world that threatens the well-being of many. Sometimes the warnings are heard by the majority, as with tornado sirens. Sometimes threats are most apparent to those marginalized by society. Sometimes it takes the voice of the committed few to alert the masses to injustices that affect the many.

In Babylonia (587-39 B.C.), Judean exiles experienced the tragedy of dislocation as well as questions of God's faithfulness, sovereignty, and will. The pain of the people was palpable.

In Isaiah 40–55 (Second Isaiah), the exilic prophet who composed the passages knew the devastation of the people. One way the author portrayed the suffering of Israel was through four servant songs (42:1-4; 49:1-6; 50:4-9; 52:13–53:12). In these songs, it is unclear whether the servant is an individual (53:1-12), Israel (50:4-9), or one in mission to Israel (49:5-6).

What the servant songs have in common is the call they present for individual/communal participation in God's purposes, even in suffering. Though defeated, Israel was to participate in God's purposes to bring "justice to the nations" (42:1). The songs claim that in God's people "God will be glorified" (49:3) as "a light to the nations" (49:6).

We, or people we care about, have probably experienced some form of suffering. Racism, ageism, sexism, and classism threaten people's ability to flourish. Illness, the death of a loved one, depression, and financial troubles threaten the lifestyle we desire. For those born in the two-thirds world in which poverty, disease, and injustice are rampant, the road of suffering is well traveled.

The servant mentioned in Isaiah provided a voice for the suffering: "The LORD God has given me the tongue of a teacher, that I may know how to sustain the weary with a word" (50:4). He also revealed the pain he had endured: "I gave my back to those who struck me, and my cheeks to those who pulled out the beard; I did not hide my face from insult and spitting" (verse 6). The servant knew what it was to suffer.

Having addressed suffering, the servant offered an alternative response to the ways in which humanity often responds to suffering. When hurt, people tend to want to hurt back. When 9/11 happened, our nation's response was to attack back. Isaiah's servant offered a different approach. Instead of retaliating with more violence, the servant refused to contribute to the cycle of violence. Instead, he bore the suffering in his body. God, who did not cause the suffering, helped the servant endure the suffering. The servant said, "The LORD God helps me; therefore I have not been disgraced" (verse 7).

Many of us have known individuals and communities who have chosen to respond to violence not with violence but by bearing the pain and suffering in their lives.

Gandhi bore the physical effects of fasting in his protest of injustice. Nelson Mandela bore the restriction and isolation of imprisonment for opposing South Africa's apartheid. Mother Teresa and fellow nuns bore the poverty and pain of the Indian people in caring for the poor in Calcutta.

The Isaiah passage continues: "Therefore I have set my face like flint, and I know that I shall not be put to shame" (verse 7). In the face of suffering and danger, God empowers those who participate in God's purposes.

In our national history, there have been persons who set their face like flint when confronting the danger and strife of oppressive circumstances. In 1965, Martin Luther King Jr. announced a march from Selma to Montgomery in the fight for blacks citizens' right to vote. When Governor George Wallace refused to permit the march, 500 marchers were beaten by state troopers. In the face of opposition and danger, the marchers "set their face like flint" as they marched with belief and integrity toward an uncertain outcome.

They did not walk alone. Selma's black citizens were joined by hundreds of blacks and whites from other states, including notable church leaders. On March 21, over 10,000 people followed King from Selma to Montgomery. Only 300 were allowed to make the 4-day march, but they were joined by 25,000 in Montgomery for the march to the capital to present a petition to Governor Wallace. The marchers made significant inroads of change. Their effort was a major factor in the passage of the Voting Rights Act that re-enfranchised black southerners. As we know, however, the journey to end racial discrimination is not yet complete. Even so, all who continue to participate in God's purposes of liberation for all will be blessed. In the words of the servant, "He who vindicates me is near" (verse 8).

The servant of the Lord confronted the threats that opposed God's purposes. He was joined by others who walked in solidarity: "Who will contend with me? Let us stand up together" (verse 8). God calls individuals to act as part of a community of faith working under the power of the Spirit to participate in God's life-giving purposes.

The servant knew that God's purposes would prevail. Those who oppose God's purposes will "wear out like a garment; the moth will eat them up" (verses 8-9). The servant had eyes to see the inroads of God's kingdom: "Every valley shall be lifted up, and every mountain and hill be made low" (40:4).

Martin Luther King Jr. also had eyes to see. His dream was shaped by God's mountaintop promises. Although King died tragically, he bore the suffering of his people even until his untimely death. King confronted the racial unjustness of an empire. Unfortunately, as Warren Carter says, "The empire always strikes back."[2]

Who in your life or your church has responded to suffering in surprising ways?

How have you or your church worked to alleviate the suffering of others?

How do you experience God's help as you participate in God's purposes?

JESUS' THREAT AND THE CONSEQUENCES OF BEING COUNTER
Mark 15:1-39

As Jesus walked his road of suffering, he set his face like flint as he confronted the threat that would lead to his death. When Jesus confronted the injustice of the empire, the empire struck back. This passage details Rome's response to the threat Jesus presented.

The plot against Jesus (3:6; 11:18; 12:12) was about to culminate in his death. The elite, who had been "looking for a way to arrest Jesus by stealth and kill him," were about to achieve their goal (14:1). Readers of Mark's Gospel who have eyes to see note that the encounter between Jesus and Rome took place at the time of Passover. The Passover evokes the Exodus, God's liberation of God's people from Egypt's empire. Those attuned to signals know the winner has already been determined.

Throughout Mark's Gospel, a distinction is made between insiders and outsiders. Those aligned with God's purposes are insiders, while those who are not are outsiders (4:10-12). The boundaries are blurred as disciples respond in fear, misunderstanding, and a lack of faith (4:38, 40; 6:49-50), while outsiders such as Jairus, a synagogue leader (5:22-43), and blind Bartimaeus (10:46-52) respond with faith. The most graphic contradiction appears when the insider Judas aligns with the powerful outsiders to betray Jesus (14:10).

Jesus gathered the disciples/insiders for the Passover meal and told them that an outsider was in their midst (14:17-18). As he broke the bread and took the cup, Jesus reiterated his purposes: "This is my blood of the covenant, which is poured out for many" (14:24). In the evoking of God's covenantal purposes, Jesus associated himself with God's liberating, life-giving covenantal purposes that have been consistent throughout the tradition (Exodus 24:8; Zechariah 9:11). Whereas Rome's purposes benefited only the few, Jesus' purposes are for "many" (14:24).

The road to the cross took Jesus and his disciples to the Mount of Olives—the place of Jesus' triumphal entry (11:1, repeated in 13:3). Take notice when words in Scripture are repeated! The Mount of Olives was a place of eschatological judgment and salvation (Zechariah 14:4), giving another signal of impending victory to an audience with eyes to see. Still, the road to the cross was arduous (14:34), paved with betrayal by insiders (14:37-51, 66-72).

The outsiders, Rome's powerful elite, continued to put their wheels of "justice" in motion as they dealt with the threat of Jesus (14:53-65). Evident in this scene are the structures through which Rome's political, military, and religious leaders implemented Rome's purposes.[3] Pilate (15:1), as provincial governor of Judea, was appointed by the emperor Tiberius to represent and enforce Rome's control by administering justice, enforcing taxation, deploying troops, and gaining cooperation through alliances made with the local political and religious elite, known as "retainers."

Retainers included the Jerusalem political, religious, and social elite who upheld Rome's systems.[4] As representatives and agents of Rome, the retainers shared in the elite's benefits and responsibilities. A primary responsibility was identifying and removing the threat of all who opposed Rome's purposes.

The threat Jesus presented came from the alternative way of life he advocated (10:41-45). Jesus' practices were counter to those of Rome. Jesus cared for those whom Rome marginalized. Jesus attacked Rome's systems by linking together "Legion," a name for a unit of Rome's army,

and demons (5:1-20). He attacked Rome's hierarchical social structure (10:42-45). In demonstrating his authority, Jesus announced judgment on the elite (12:1-11, 38-40) and predicted the downfall of the Temple, a primary place Rome's unjust economic systems were implemented.[5]

It is no surprise that representatives of the Roman elite—retainers, including the high priest, chief priests, elders, and scribes—gathered to deal with the threat Jesus presented (14:53-66). Still Jesus refused to play the game the way Rome wanted it played. He refused to submit to Rome's authority. Instead of answering questions, he quoted Daniel 7:13 and Psalm 110:1 and identified himself as "the Christ," God's appointed representative. His references to Daniel and the Psalms evoked scenes of God's power and judgment. Jesus was asserting that God's empire—not Rome's— would triumph! (14:62). Rome, however, asserted that Rome was all powerful. Clearly, the two empires were at cross-purposes. The council determined Jesus was a case for the governor and handed him over to Pilate (15:1).

It would appear that Jesus being "handed over" to a Roman governor indicated Rome's control. For those with eyes to see, however, the verb "handed over" is revealing. Jesus used this verb three times in Mark to predict his death (9:31, translated as "betrayed," and twice in 10:33). If it is repeated, take notice! Though it appeared that the Roman government was in control, Jesus knew what was happening. Those with eyes to see know that God is in control.

Although Pilate is often portrayed as weak or indecisive, he was neither. Pilate was a cunning, shrewd politician. By asking questions of the crowd, he was determining the level of threat the people presented. The Roman government did not want a riot on its hands (14:2). Pilate was determining how easily the crowd could be manipulated to serve Rome's purposes.

I wish I could say that I was innocent of using language and timing to achieve my purposes, but I am a mom. At times, I must avail myself of the tools I have at hand. Often, my sons will ask for a privilege—often one that involves money and time and has no immediately apparent benefit to their humanity. Sometimes I will respond with "We'll see." Their reaction alerts me to the importance of the event. A delay in my response allows me to frame the discussion on my terms.

Pilate's encounter with the crowd was completely on his and Rome's terms. In his political astuteness, he did not make this clear to the crowd, who felt because of the questioning that they had a voice in the decision that Roman authorities had already made. The decision to put Jesus to death, a decision made long ago (3:6; 11:18; 12:2; 14:1-2), was put into action. Jesus was "handed over" to be crucified (15:15).

On Jesus' road to death, the blur between insiders and outsiders continued. The disciples, insiders, abandoned Jesus at Gethsemane (14:32-42). Judas betrayed Jesus (14:43). Disciples fled (14:50). Even Peter betrayed Jesus (14:66-72).

Conversely, apparent outsiders turned out to be insiders of God's empire. Simon of Cyrene carried Jesus' cross (15:21). The Gentile centurion revealed Jesus' identity as "truly . . . God's Son" (verse 39). Women, though marginalized by society, remained faithful (verses 40-41), as did Joseph of Arimathea, a member of the Jerusalem Council, in a brazen encounter with Pilate (verse 43).

Mark's Passion story indicates that where you stand determines what you see. If you see as ultimate the power of empires that oppress many to benefit a few, you may well be outside God's empire. If, on the other hand, you participate in God's reversal of society in which "every valley shall be lifted up, and every mountain and hill be made low" (Isaiah 40:4), you have an insider's view of God's empire.

Living an alternative existence requires that we recognize the systems that are contrary to God's purposes. It means that we recognize signals of distress so that we can contribute to God's purpose to care for others as well as ourselves. It requires that we "set our faces like flint" and participate in life-giving, loving, liberating efforts that bring about life-giving change.

Timmy, my 11-year-old, recently observed: "Mom," he said, "When you say, 'We'll see,' it always ends up being 'no.' " He is catching on! The more we catch on to the signs of God's kingdom that is at hand, the more "we'll see" signs of God's empire that are God's ultimate "yes" to the flourishing of creation.

What structures in your life, church, and society seem contrary to God's purposes? Which ones contribute to God's purposes?

What people, places, feelings, or activities in your life threaten your participation in God's purposes?

What people, places, feelings, or activities inform or inspire your participation in God's purposes?

What signs and signals of God's empire do you see in the midst of your everyday life?

---

[1]From "Constructing the Roman Imperial System" in *Matthew and Empire: Initial Explorations* (Trinity Press International, 2001); pages 9-19, and *New Testament and Negotiating the Roman Imperial World*, by Warren Carter (Abingdon Press, 2006).
[2]From *Matthew and the Margins: A Sociopolitical Reading*, by Warren Carter (Orbis Books, 2000); pages 73-89.
[3]From *Hearing the Whole Story: The Politics of Plot in Mark's Gospel*, by Richard A. Horsley (Westminster John Knox Press, 2001); pages 27-52.
[4]From *Pontius Pilate: Portraits of a Roman Governor*, by Warren Carter (Liturgical Press, 2003); pages 35-54.
[5]*Jesus, Justice, and the Reign of God: A Ministry of Liberation*, by William R. Herzog II (Westminster John Knox Press, 2000); pages 111-43.

The Difference a Vision Can Make

Scriptures for Easter:
Isaiah 25:6-9
Mark 16:1-8
Acts 10:34-43

We have made it through the darkness of Good Friday and the waiting of the Easter vigil to the glory of Easter morning. Unlike the first witnesses to Jesus' crucifixion, who huddled in hiding not knowing what the future held, we know the victory that is coming. Even in the bleakness of Good Friday, the glory of Easter looms.

Circumstances often make it difficult for people to picture a future brighter than the bleakness of the present. Even in the darkest times, though, God's vision for a loving, liberating reality breaks through. In Isaiah 25:6-9, we see God's vision of abundance for all. In Mark 16:1-8, the women's response to Jesus' resurrection shows how difficult it can be to live out God's vision. In Acts 10:34-43, Peter proclaims the good news of God's vision for all.

We know that where we stand determines what we see. Today, we stand on this side of the Resurrection. As Resurrection people, we claim the good news: "Christ is risen." In the light of the Resurrection, we can confidently watch and joyfully pray for ways to live into God's vision for and actions toward the flourishing of all creation.

A VISION OF GOD'S EMPIRE
Isaiah 25:6-9

When my sister was training to run a marathon, she told our family that in addition to her physical preparation, she was preparing mentally. "By getting your head examined?" my dad asked, unable to understand why anyone would want to run 26.2 miles. Susan frowned and explained that she was practicing "visualization." Visualization involves mentally rehearsing positive outcomes of future events. Susan said her repeated envisioning of herself running strong and fast along her course helped train her mind for the rigors of marathon day. Before she could run the course, she had to believe it was possible. Visualization made a difference.

The Book of Isaiah begins with a vision: "The vision of Isaiah son of Amoz ..." (1:1). The prophet received his call through a vision (6:1-13) that cast its light over its contents. The book is framed in terms of judgment and salvation. Exile is interpreted as God's judgment on God's disobedient people. Judgment, though, is not the final word. The overriding message is one of salvation.

You may be wondering what this has to do with Easter. Easter is about the resurrection of Christ, which happened centuries later. For Christians, the Resurrection enacts God's vision of life, love, liberation, and salvation even from the powers of death. This mighty act is not a new thought for God. It is consistent with God's purposes of and promises for universal salvation expressed throughout Scripture.

We know that God's purposes for life, love, and liberation are lived out *within* history. The question before us is, What does the Resurrection mean for us at this juncture in history? In living this question, it is helpful to reflect on Isaiah's thoughts about God's purposes in history.

While the Book of Isaiah did not receive its final form until after the Exile (587-39 B.C.), it contains material from over three centuries, beginning in the eighth century B.C. Though the circumstances changed through the centuries, Israel faced constant challenges as they lived amidst successive oppressive powers (Assyria in the eighth century and Babylon in the sixth century B.C.). What is the overriding vision or message that emerges? How can Isaiah's vision shed light on life today as we negotiate powers that oppose God's purposes?

We know what it is to experience powers that want our allegiance—the power of money and material goods, of status, of patriotism, of addictive pleasures. Isaiah asserts that God can be trusted to deliver God's people from all the powers that oppose God's purposes. The final form of Isaiah 25:6-9 is believed to have been shaped during and after Babylonian exile. By this time, the Temple was destroyed; and the Holy City, Jerusalem, was in ruins. Even in the darkness of their circumstances, "a few survivors" of faith (1:9) continued to believe in God's sovereignty and faithfulness. They offered God praise in the midst of their exile: "I will exalt you. I will praise your name; for you have done wonderful things" (25:1). .

Survivors of faith trust in God's sovereignty and faithfulness because they know God's nature and purposes: "For you have been a refuge to the poor, a refuge to the needy in their distress, a shelter from the rainstorm and a shade from the heat" (verse 4).

Survivors of faith look beyond today and recognize God's beckoning tomorrow. What does the promise of God's coming realm look like? Isaiah offers a vision.

Isaiah pointed to a future on "this mountain" (verse 6). "This mountain" refers to the Temple Mount in Jerusalem, the holy place of encounter between God and humankind (2:2-3). Isaiah's vision was one of hope, of seeing beyond the state of the decimated Temple to the transformation of tomorrow. There, "the LORD of hosts will make for all peoples a feast of rich food, a feast of well-aged wines, of rich food filled with marrow, of well-aged wines strained clear" (25:6). A joyous celebration requires the best of food (Deuteronomy 14:26; Luke 15:23). While in exile, survivors of faith envisioned the abundance of God's provision. Even in their lack, they knew that God's plan was for plenty.

Unlike in Isaiah's time in which abundance was given only to the 2-5 percent elite, God's generosity extends to "all peoples" (Isaiah 25:6). From the beginning, it has been God's plan to bless "all the families of the earth" (Genesis 12:3). Accordingly, in the end, it is God's plan that all peoples shall partake in the abundance of God's gifts (Isaiah 66:18).

In Isaiah's time, as in our own, suffering and death were a present reality. In addition to the mental and physical hardships caused by the elite's oppression of the peasant population (Chapter 5), wars caused extensive suffering, death, and devastation.[1] Isaiah asserted that suffering is not part of God's vision: God "will destroy on this mountain the shroud that is cast over all peoples, the sheet that is spread over all nations; he will swallow up death forever. Then the Lord GOD will wipe away the tears from all faces, and the disgrace of his people he will take away from all the earth, for the LORD has spoken" (25:7-8). Those who trust in God will be rewarded. They will see face to face the God they have trusted: "This is the LORD for whom we have waited; let us be glad and rejoice in his salvation" (verse 9). Those with eyes to see recognize God's purposes and promises as a present reality.

My sister said that as she ran in the hot sun, she imagined the finish line and the post-race spread of oranges, bananas, yogurt, and bagels with lots of fresh ice water. Susan's vision did not include just herself. She had been training with a dozen friends who gathered every Saturday—rain, shine, or snow—to run their 10-, 15-, or 20-mile training runs. Envisioning all of them at the finish helped negotiate the heat and hills. My sister's vision of finishing the marathon became a reality. Everyone in her running group finished. Afterward, they found a shady tree and celebrated their victory with a feast of oranges, bananas, and ice cream bars.

I feel it is important to add that my sister ran the marathon as a hobby. There are many in the world, however, for whom leisure is not an option. Much of the world's population is spending its energy trying to survive. There are more than 800 million people who are chronically undernourished. More than half the world's children (more than 1 billion) are suffering extreme deprivations from poverty, war, and HIV/AIDS.[2] In the US, a baby is born into poverty every 14 seconds; and 11 percent of households experience hunger. Nearly one fourth of American workers earn too little to meet their family's basic needs, with 34.6 million living at or below the poverty level.

Today, as in Isaiah's time, an uneven distribution of God's gifts causes those who live on inadequate resources to suffer inordinately. Lack of food, inadequate housing, and lack of medical care lead to hardship, disease, and early death. The suffering that results is not in God's plan for anyone.

It does not have to be this way. Millard Fuller envisioned a way to build modest houses on a no-profit, no-interest basis. He wanted to make homes affordable to families with low incomes. After moving to Africa with his wife and four children to test the housing concept, they decided it was a vision worth implementing. Millard and Linda Fuller went on to create Habitat for Humanity International in 1976. As of 2005, Habitat has provided homes for more than 1 million people. Of their accomplishments, Linda says, "To families in seemingly impossible situations, Habitat for Humanity becomes a friend and partner. And, by their own labor and with God's grace, they become owners of a decent home."[3] One man's vision, illuminated by God's grace, has changed a million people's lives.

By participating in God's purposes for the flourishing of creation, the faithful not only survive but also thrive. As Isaiah of Babylon promises, "Those who wait for the LORD shall renew their strength, they shall mount up with wings like eagles, they shall run and not be weary, they shall walk and not faint" (40:31).

What would it mean for you to receive the abundance of God's grace?

Is there anything in your life that you would like God to destroy?

How is your church working with God for the good of "all peoples"?

SEEING THROUGH EYES OF FEAR OR FAITH
Mark 16:1-8

In Mark 14–15, circumstances for Jesus and his followers were bleak. Jesus, after having gone through the trial before Pilate, was put to death by crucifixion, a tortuous, horrific means of execution.

In Mark 16, female followers of Jesus were going to the tomb to anoint Jesus (verses 1-3). When they arrived at Jesus' tomb, though, the stone that covered the entrance had already been rolled back (verse 4). A "young man, dressed in a white robe" (verse 5) announced: "Do not be alarmed; you are looking for Jesus of Nazareth, who was crucified. He has been raised; he is not here" (verse 6). The Resurrection story in Mark is the story of the empty tomb, the proof that Jesus was raised by God.

Mark's Gospel opens with "the beginning of the good news of Jesus Christ, the Son of God" (1:1). The end of the Gospel reveals the full extent of the good news. Throughout the Gospel, Jesus had lived out his claim that "the kingdom of God has come near" (1:15). Jesus had shown that the good news of God's empire (1:15) consists of the sick being healed (1:29-34), the hungry being fed 6:30-44; 8:1-10), and demons being exorcized (1:21-28). Jesus' manifestation of God's empire caused people to show allegiance to God's purposes, which were contrary to Rome's purposes (14:1-2). Accordingly, Rome had Jesus crucified.

Crucifixion, though, is not the end of the story. The good news of Mark's Gospel is that the worst that Roman power could do was no match for God's power. Rome caused Jesus' death. God raised Jesus from the dead, demonstrating that God's power was sovereign over Rome's. The purposes of Jesus' earthly ministry—feeding, healing, caring for God's people—were vindicated in and through his resurrection. The question is, Who has eyes to recognize and participate in God's purposes?

Mark acknowledged that discipleship is hard work. In difficult times, it can be difficult even to envision God's purposes, let alone find ways to participate. Still, Mark encouraged faithful discipleship even and especially in difficult times.

In the end, despite all that Jesus taught and demonstrated, the disciples in Mark did not see their commitments through. They all abandoned Jesus: "All of them deserted him and fled" (14:50; see also 32-42, 43, 66-72). The good news, though, is there were those who recognized and participated in God's purposes. Though not official disciples, their actions and attitudes made them insiders to God's kingdom or empire. Simon of Cyrene carried Jesus' cross (15:21). After the Crucifixion, the Gentile centurion said, "Truly this man was God's Son!" (15:39). The women "look[ed] on from a distance" (15:40). Joseph of Arimathea, a member of the council, asked Pilate for the body of Jesus (15:43).

In Mark 16, the women first received the good news of the empty tomb and the instructions,

"Go, tell his disciples and Peter that he is going ahead of you to Galilee; there you will see him, just as he told you" (verse 7). Did the women abandon Jesus like the disciples did? Were they faithful like the non-disciples who recognized the significance of Jesus? Mark saved the drama until the end. As it turns out, it was not a happy ending: "So they went out and fled from the tomb, for terror and amazement had seized them; and they said nothing to anyone, for they were afraid (verse 8). (Verse 8 was the original ending to Mark. A longer ending [verses 9-20] was added in the late second or early third century A.D.)

Why would the original author end the Gospel at 16:8? What good news is there to an ending that had almost everyone abandon Jesus? Scholars think Mark ended this way in order to motivate the hearers or the readers into faithful discipleship. Mark shows that none of those who should have been faithful—the disciples and the women—carried out Jesus' vision. Only Jesus was faithful to God's purposes, even unto death. Only God was faithful to defeat death and raise up Jesus.

The message of Mark is that in the hardship and suffering of faithful discipleship, in participation with God's purposes, the faithful encounter the risen Christ. Good news, indeed.

The question Mark leaves us with is, Will we respond to the challenges of faithful discipleship with fear or with faith?

Why do you think the disciples and the women responded with fear?

What is there to fear about faithful discipleship today?

How can we as individuals and as the church experience the Resurrection today?

LIVING INTO GOD'S VISION
Acts 10:34-43

My sister decided to run her marathon despite her trepidation. We all rejoiced with her when she crossed the finish line—running strong, beating her goal. Susan will be the first to tell you that visualization was only part of her success. The rest had to do with six months of disciplined, consistent training. Visualization helped her to see what to do; training made her capable of actually doing it.

Our last passage takes us to the Acts of the Apostles. Written by the author of Luke, Acts gives a narrative account of the early church, from the ascension of Jesus to the spread of the gospel "to the ends of the earth" (1:8). In Acts 10:34-43, Peter shares the good news of the risen Christ with the Gentiles. Even as Peter was *sharing* the good news, he was learning what it meant to *live* the good news. It meant doing things differently than they had been done before.

As a faithful Jew, Peter adhered to strict food laws. There were "clean" foods to eat and "unclean" foods to avoid. A faithful Jew could not share the table with Gentiles. To abandon Jewish food practices would have meant abandoning one of the three distinctive marks of Jewish identity (the others being circumcision and sabbath observance).

God had a different vision for how Jewish followers of Jesus were to live. God's vision was that the faithful would not be divided between insiders and outsiders. God's empire is all-inclusive. As in the mountain vision in Isaiah, "all peoples" are called to be together at the table.

In Acts 10, Cornelius and Peter received visions. Cornelius was a Roman soldier who feared God, gave alms generously, and prayed constantly (verses 2, 22, 31). God responded to Cornelius's faithful practices with a vision. He was to "send men to Joppa for a certain Simon who is called Peter" (verse 5). Meanwhile, Peter was praying (verse 9) and probably fasting (verse 10) when he received a vision. In Peter's vision, he was to "kill and eat" what according to his faith was "unclean" (verses 13-15). This happened three times! (If it is repeated, sit up and take notice!)

In a wonderful convergence of visions, as Peter was contemplating the meaning of his vision, the men sent by Cornelius appeared. Peter invited them in, presumably sharing a table with these Gentiles (verse 23). The next day, Peter and the men from Joppa came to see Cornelius. Peter said, "You yourselves know that it is unlawful for a Jew to associate with or to visit a Gentile; but God has shown me that I should not call anyone profane or unclean. So when I was sent for, I came without objection" (verses 28-29). While Cornelius and Peter were praying, they had visions that caused them to begin living life differently. Both crossed existing boundaries. Both took risks of faith to live out the vision of God's inclusive love.

Obedience to God's vision set the stage for Peter's delivery of the good news in verses 34-43. Because of their faithful risk-taking, Cornelius and other believers were "in the presence of God to listen to all that the Lord has commanded [Peter] to say" (verse 33).

Peter said, "I truly understand that God shows no partiality, but in every nation anyone who fears him and does what is right is acceptable to him" (verses 34-35). Peter's previous actions showed that he understood God's vision and faithfully put it into practice when he showed the men from Joppa hospitality and then traveled with them to Cornelius.

Peter went on to show that he understood the meaning of the Resurrection. By raising Jesus from the dead, God vindicated all that Jesus did in his lifetime. Peter noted how Jesus "went about doing good and healing all who were oppressed by the devil, for God was with him" (verse 38). Peter knew the power of God to conquer even death (verse 40). Further, Peter knew the privilege and responsibility that witnessing God's purposes entailed (verses 41-43). The good news is not to be kept to oneself. It is to be shared by participating in God's purposes to bring God's vision into reality.

Peter and Cornelius saw God's vision because they participated in faithful practices. They performed consistent, disciplined practices of faith—prayer, meditation, and fasting—so that they could be in position to be blessed. The Fullers were living lives of faithful discipline when they started Habitat for Humanity. Disciplines of faith put us in position to recognize and live the message of the Resurrection.

Like Peter and Cornelius, Millard and Linda Fuller made significant life changes in responding to God's call on their lives. Before founding Habitat for Humanity, Millard had risen from humble beginnings to become a successful millionaire by age 29. Success took a toll on his health, well-being, and his marriage. Soul searching led him to recommit himself to Christ and to his wife. The Fullers took a significant risk by selling their possessions, giving their money to the poor, and moving to a Christian community where people tried to be intentional in living out Christ's teach-

ings. Their faithful practices put them in a position to implement God's vision towards the flourishing of all.

It is said that seeing is believing. It can also be said that believing teaches us how to see. Once we see God's purposes, we can watch and pray for ways to participate in God's purposes. It is in participating in God's purposes that we experience resurrection in our lives, our churches, and our world.

Hear the good news: Christ is risen, indeed!

What does the Resurrection mean for you in your life? in the life of your church?

How is your life different as a Christian than it would be if you were not?

How does God's vision for life, love, and liberation look in your life? in your church? in your community? in the world?

---

[1]Wars during the composition of Isaiah included the Syro-Ephraimite war (735-32 B.C.), the rebellion King Hezekiah led against Assyria (705-01 B.C.), the Assyrian invasion of Judah (701 B.C.), and the Babylonian invasion of Jerusalem (587 B.C.).
[2]From "Childhood Under Threat" in *The State of the World's Children 2005 at http://www.unicef.org/sowc05/english/childhoodunderthreat.html.*
[3]From Linda Fuller at *http://www.habitat.org/how/linda.html.*